Dear Mrs. Jannice,  P9-DNB-740

I hope this doesn't make you unpleasant and you understand me. I would like to write you and be friendly and write your girl, too. I know her from her picture her daddy show me, and I would like to send her some nice things sometime.

I love her daddy and he loves me, too. I don't know why. It is my fate. I hope you tell me what he likes and how to make him happy. He loved you and was happy. Maybe we can make each other peaceful.

Please say best regard to your other children for me, and tell them that the war in Vietnam will be over some day soon, and perhaps we shall all be together as one. It would be nice if we could see the peace together, your country and mine.

Love,
Diep

PAPER BRIDGES:
From Vietnam With Love

PAPER BRIDGES

from Vietnam With Love

by
Jann Jansen

Ⓞ
A SIGNET BOOK

SIGNET
Published by the Penguin Group
Penguin Books, USA Inc., 375 Hudson Street,
New York, New York 10014, U.S.A.
Penguin Books Ltd, 27 Wrights Lane,
London W8 5TZ, England
Penguin Books Australia Ltd, Ringwood,
Victoria, Australia
Penguin Books Canada Ltd, 2801 John Street,
Markham, Ontario, Canada L3R 1B4
Penguin Books (N.Z.) Ltd, 182-190 Wairau Road,
Auckland 10, New Zealand

Penguin Books Ltd, Registered Offices:
Harmondsworth, Middlesex, England

First Published by Signet, an imprint of New American Library,
a division of Penguin Books USA Inc.

First Printing, January 1991
10 9 8 7 6 5 4 3 2 1

Ⓞ REGISTRED TRADEMARK—MARCA REGISTRADA

Printed in the United States of America

Almost over eighteen years we had just contacted by the letters, and there are hundreds and hundreds of letters over the Pacific Ocean to me and to Jannice. We came to another by the letters, and now we will be face to face. . . . What will be the first second we meet? I know she will be at the airport waiting—I am confused!

—Nguyen Thi Diep, May 16, 1985

Chapter One

Women of Two Cultures, Linked by One Man

We've known each other well, although we have never met.

Soon, Nguyen Thi Diep and I will be face to face for the first time, after over eighteen years of correspondence. We are both a little scared. Diep and I have shared experiences and feelings with an intimacy often missed by the closest friends.

Ours has been a friendship that grew in spite of my initial hesitancy. When it began, she and I were young women and our countries were engaged in a terrible war. The year was 1966. Over the years, we developed a closeness that transcended both geographic and language barriers. Our friendship endured throughout Diep's ten years of struggle in the New Economic Zone following the fall of Saigon, and it survived the enforced silence between us when the Communist takeover began.

Over three hundred letters traveled the sixteen-thousand-mile distance between our countries, paper bridges that linked our cultures.

When I finally decided to answer one of her "letters of friendly" so many years ago, she responded by sending two beautiful *ao-dai* (Vietnamese dresses) for my daughters. My letter of thanks was followed by another letter from her.

I soon learned that she was the mother of two half-American baby girls, children of different fathers, and that she worked as a librarian for the U.S. Army based in Da Nang, South Vietnam.

As the newly separated mother of five small children, I was struggling on a piano teacher's meager earnings to support my children. The youngest had recently been diagnosed as having cystic fibrosis, a chronic lung disorder.

Diep's first letter of introduction, addressed to my eldest daughter, had been cordial and polite, but somewhat timid. In it, she sought only friendship from her lover's family. At the time, I had thought it inappropriate to respond since the man in her life was my estranged husband.

"Here they come, the refugees!" someone exclaimed at the ramp leading from the plane. An NBC-TV affiliate reporter, having read one of my articles about my relationship with Diep, was there with his cameraman. He wanted an interview. Two airport employees went aboard the plane at my request to warn Diep. I was afraid that after all she had been through so recently, such attention might alarm her. When the airport officials learned that the television newsman was there with his crew, I was allowed to wait beyond the customs and outside gates.

The first people off the Northwest Orient plane were in wheelchairs, escorted by airport attendants. Then came Vietnamese and Cambodian children, many of them burned or badly disfigured from old injuries, then elderly people assisted by younger adults, then two Cambodians bent double under the weight of the crudely tied boxes on their backs, followed by many men and women who seemed ill or tired; all flooded around me as I waited near the ramp.

Anxiety, an electric tension, was in the air as people continued to file out of the plane. Some were greeted by sponsors, others gazed anxiously about in fear and confusion, while still other refugees huddled together, speaking in their soft, lilting language, perhaps offering words of comfort and reassurance to each other.

Two flight attendants stood near me, laughing, as I anxiously looked for Diep and her daughters. Would we recognize each other? Or would they somehow manage to pass by me, and would we lose each other once again?

One of the flight attendants moved closer to me so two very elderly Vietnamese women and a young child could pass.

"One Cambodian couple actually thought that America was all paved with cement," she explained to me as her friend continued giggling. "Before they boarded, we had to confiscate some bags of cow manure they'd collected during their detention in the Philippines."

I looked puzzled.

"Don't you see?" she said, laughing again. "The man believed there was no dirt here, and that he'd have to bring his own fertilizer and soil to plant his garden."

I wondered then what misconceptions Diep might have about this country, and if she would feel comfortable telling me about them. Then I saw her. Her daughters, Jeanie (Mai-Cat) and Jolie (Mai-Uyen), were close by her side. Except for Diep's hand-embroidered Vietnamese blouse, their clothes were Western, Diep in dark brown pants and her daughters in turtleneck sweaters with matching short skirts.

Jeanie immediately put her arms around my neck and wept; Jolie stood close by, smiling with embarrassment and holding back her tears. Diep, frail and tired, extended her hand and delivered a little rehearsed speech of gratitude. As Jeanie clung to me tearfully, I sensed that they were all relieved. Later I learned that they had heard many stories about sponsors abandoning refugees, and they feared I might have second thoughts and not show up.

"I told my girls that you would be here," Diep said, "but they were not so sure. They say: 'Why Mrs. Jannice help us? Why she do this for us?' I say that you are good and kind, and that we have been like sisters for many years. You would not turn your back on us, I say."

During the trip across the Bay Bridge toward home, a thirty-mile drive, each of us seemed lost in our own thoughts. The girls spoke to each other occasionally in Vietnamese, and Diep replied falteringly to my questions. Familiar sights took on freshness as I tried to imagine how they looked to these newcomers. It was as though I looked at everything with new eyes.

Later Jolie told me: "We have a new name when we come here—'refugee.' In America, refugee's first step of new life is very difficult: no house, no job, nothing. I knew that many hard things would come in my new life. I knew, but I was not afraid. I have my hands, my feet, my mind. I can work to live. I still have the loves from you. . . . On the way home from the airport, I saw everyone seemed quiet, each people had private thinking. What did you think about us? I wanted to speak, but my English wasn't enough to speak. My mother didn't speak to you much. I knew she was too nervous."

When we got home, I realized that Diep was not feeling

well. When my husband and I showed her the large room that she and her daughters would share, she suddenly sank to her knees. I was frightened. Had she fainted? Her daughters looked worried but were silent. I asked Jeanie, the older one, if her mother had been ill aboard the plane. She didn't understand me. It was at that moment that I realized the girls barely spoke English and understood very little of the language as well. The letters I had received from Jeanie over the years must have been written with an English/Vietnamese dictionary in hand and labored over tediously.

Diep insisted that she would be all right. Fatigue, excitement, and fear had all contributed to her sudden collapse. I made up the beds, brought her some hot tea and an aspirin, and left them alone.

The following morning found the trio bright-eyed and looking much happier. Diep had recovered, and together we began to review the past that for so many years had been chronicled in our letters to each other.

We found we had far more in common than just the shared relationship with my first husband, Ed Whittemore. Both of us had struggled to take care of our families, and both of us had valued our educations when young. Both of us were intensely loyal.

Wednesday's Child, I was born on an overcast day in April. Mary Charlene, my demure, fragile mother, was a sad and complex woman. Her dark hair framed a fine-boned oval face, and her green eyes—Asian lidded—forever registered her innate distrust of mankind. The love-hate she felt for my father, George Bernard, was of such hot intensity that, had she been violently inclined, he never would have known a safe moment.

My father was a handsome, dark-eyed charmer whose

attraction to women was equally matched by their attraction to him. For a time, his social ease and winning warmth compensated for my mother's shyness and detachment, until her insecurity finally undid whatever balance could be found in their mismatched union.

She was a brooding Vivien Leigh look-alike; he could have been a second Errol Flynn. They met and married in Oakland, California, where I was born. For a young woman who had helped rear two brothers and a younger sister, marriage to this fun-loving, irresponsible, foot-loose man soon became intolerable. He was impulsive, sensitive, fearless, passionate, and unpredictable, and the desperate need for roots and stability that my mother battled to achieve was never to be satisfied by him.

My father had been a pilot with the Flying Tigers in World War Two, but he was a dreamer as well, a man who was always sure that one day an oil well would be found in his back yard, or a rich vein of gold discovered on property left to him by some mysterious benefactor. His life was marked by the chaos that comes from the volatile combination of unfounded optimism and unchartered daring. He lived out some of his fantasies, but those fantasies that promised stability and security were beyond either his desire or his reach. His stint with the Flying Tigers was perhaps the only time when his daredevil inclinations found an acceptable outlet.

Mother had untapped talents, but motherhood was not one of them. She had to work. That was a necessity. When I was just a baby, she placed me with an older couple, Peggy and Warner Semple, who were our upstairs neighbors, and proceeded to move away, taking a job with MacFarlane's Candy Company in Berkeley.

Father simply decamped. My last memory of him was when I was about five and he came to visit me at the

Semples' home. Young as I was, I somehow knew that I would never see him again.

The Semples, in their late fifties, were childless until I came into their lives. I stayed with them for seven years, occasionally seeing my mother on Wednesdays. Their love of me was demonstrated daily, whether with kindly instruction, leisurely evening baths followed by bedtime stories, or time spent carefully braiding my pigtails, all testimonials to their love and caring, as was my occasionally being chased upstairs with a hairbrush tapping at my derriere when I had misbehaved. Whatever their parental controls, I was always aware that they loved me unconditionally.

When I was seven, my mother remarried, to a man with a genius as undisciplined as my father's passion for life had been.

I can never forget my grief that day when my mother and this stranger who reeked of tobacco took me away from the Semples, away from my light, airy bedroom with my socks and hair ribbons neatly folded in the dresser drawers. I wanted to die, unable to articulate the wish but miserable enough to know even at that young age how to carry it out. After two weeks of not eating and crying myself to sleep every night, I became so ill that the doctor advised my furious mother and stepfather to return me "for a short time" to the Semples' home. They did, but neither I nor my beloved Peggy and Warner, who had been parents to me, would ever be forgiven for it.

When I returned to live with my mother, I was forbidden to have any further contact with the Semples. I remained in mourning for a long time. I will never forget how I dreaded recesses during those first few months when I was enrolled in a new school. The Semples, grieving over our separation, often parked near the school yard in the hope of catching a glimpse of me, but my parents had a firm rule that we were not to speak to each other or touch. "Contact will only make the break harder," they explained. So I would hide on the basement steps leading to the custodian's closets until I saw the Semples' car pull away slowly, taking with it memories of the warm security of a house that smelled of freshly baked cookies and warm hugs meant just for me.

My new home was quite different. Dave, my mother's new husband, saw in me a talent and intelligence he regarded as an interesting challenge, and the artist in him—he was a frustrated painter—was moved to develop this child into an image of himself. My piano lessons, which had begun when I was five and Mother and Dave were courting, were their greatest gift to me. But any nurturing, outside of providing those necessities required for life, was beyond their capabilities.

When I went to live with Mother and Dave, the cuddling I had craved and received from Peggy and Warner Semple became only a memory. Hugging my mother was like hugging a chair. The only difference was that a chair doesn't pull away.

Lucky is the child who can find acceptance in such a home. I was fortunate to have musical ability, which made Mother and Dave proud of me. By the age of seven, I was already playing Bach and Mozart and losing myself in my music.

I was a shy little girl, torn between loyalties for the aging and loving Semples and the pretty woman I was directed to call "Mother," whose love for classical music led me to a new dream of becoming a concert pianist.

At nine I contracted tuberculosis, and for over two years my world was contained within one room. I was isolated from the outside and from school friends and tutored by my stepfather. I would return to public school with the vocabulary of a well-read adult. Dave had assigned me books by Dickens, Twain, Robert Lewis Stevenson, Steinbeck, Hemingway, and other major writers, but the price for this wondrous gift of knowledge was that I was now a misfit among my peers. I found solace in my world of books and in music, and by the time I was in my second year of high school I already had a lucrative job giving piano lessons.

I went away to college to the Conservatory of Music at University of Pacific. Too young to have left home, I was now lost in the true sense. Suffering from a severe case of homesickness, I was probably one of the cleanest co-eds on campus, since I spent many hours that first semester taking showers, sobbing out my loneliness, where no one could hear me. It was only natural, I suppose, that I would respond to the constant attentions of another student who attended school, an ex-Marine, veteran of the Korean War, named Ed Whittemore.

He never let me out of his sight. I lived in the dormitory and he lived off campus, yet he was always waiting for me when I left for classes in the morning, and he somehow managed to see me throughout each day and every evening. Since he also lived in Oakland, when I did visit my home on occasional weekends he went with me to visit his own family, as well as to be with me. I was partly flattered and partly afraid of this intense relationship. My parents were vehemently opposed to it.

"If you continue to see this man," my stepfather told me, "I'm going to cut off your support. There's absolutely no reason for you to go to college, especially the Conservatory, if marriage is in your plans."

It wasn't, but I continued seeing my persistent suitor, and my stepfather was true to his word and cut off both my tuition and support. Since it was impossible for me to support myself and pay the high tuition at the university, too, I went to work with the hope of perhaps saving up enough money so that I could return the following semester. But the pay was poor, and since better-paying work was hard to find, I was forced to give up my dreams of college.

The alienation from my parents became worse. As they now threatened to disown me, even disinherit me if I continued to date Ed, I fled to the comfort and "security" of his arms. My parents' rejection was balanced by Ed's total acceptance at a time when there was very little ballast in my life. Of course I had options, but in my hurt and confusion I could not see them, and the idea of striking out on my own was terrifying.

We married at the end of my first year at college. My parents remained unbending and refused to attend the simple ceremony at a neighborhood chapel. "You have just flushed your musical career and all of our investment in it down the toilet," my mother said the day before my marriage. This was her main justification for closing her door to me.

Within nine and a half months my first baby was born, a little girl we named Donice. It marked my own rebirth, for I would never recall her birth without experiencing a joyful thrill. She and the other children who followed filled a creative void for me, providing me with a clear-cut definition of who I was and what my role was to be during that time in my life. It was a role I could understand, a fulfilling role, and one I could accomplish well.

My second child, a blond and blue-eyed boy we named Chris, was born two years later in Berkeley, California. By now, with the financial help of Ed's brother, we were able to buy a home in a quiet, tree-shaded older neighborhood where I was the youngest wife/mother of all. Some of the other ladies took me under their wings, regarding me as a naive child who had much to learn. One of them was to become my closest friend.

"Hello, I'm Dottie Hahn, your neighbor from down the street." The woman who introduced herself to me on that crisp spring morning was about ten years older than I, a Clairol blonde with sharp features and an Eveready smile. I probably registered disbelief at her attire—a bathrobe—and seeing the empty coffee cup clutched in her hand made me laugh.

"Well, my husband just left for work, and I wanted to meet you anyway. You *do* drink coffee, don't you?" she asked amiably.

"Yes, but all I have is instant," I said apologetically. "Come inside before you freeze."

"Is this your second baby?" Dottie asked, nodding toward my pregnant form. I told her it was baby number three.

"You've been moved in now about how long? Two months at least? I planned to stop by long ago, but you know how those things go."

She was outgoing and friendly, and we talked for several hours until she decided it was time to go home and make the beds. "Besides," she said as she walked out the door, "I hate to have the mailman come to my house and see me in this tattered old robe. He's pretty cute. Have you seen him?"

"Yes, but I never noticed." I smiled.

"NOTICE!" she said authoritatively, a tone I would often hear in her voice in the years to come. Later it was Dottie who drove me to the hospital to have my baby, and as she waited for ten hours through my labor and delivery, our friendship-bonding really took place.

"What does that old man of yours do, anyway?" she asked one afternoon. "Spill his seed and then get on with business as usual?"

"Dottie! That's awful!"

"Well, he's shown you and the new kid about as much attention as a tomcat shows his litter. And that baby boy's a real cutie, too."

Without realizing it, she was getting close to discovering my painful secret: My husband and I were having troubles.

By the time our third child, Warner, was nine months old, I knew that I would have to prepare myself for a more profitable occupation than the piano teaching I had been doing all along. Teaching school had always been a dream of mine, so I enrolled in classes at Diablo Valley College three mornings a week.

"You're preparing yourself for being on your own one day, aren't you?" Dottie blurted out suddenly one morning as she was drinking coffee and I was folding laundry. "I mean, this college thing . . . that's what it's about?"

"It's not exactly preparing myself for divorce," I said slowly. "It's just a smart idea in case it ever comes down to that."

"Hey, this is Dottie who loves ya'," she said. "Yours isn't exactly one of those marriages made in heaven."

"Is there such a thing?"

"What a cynic we've become," she said, tucking her chin in and rolling her eyes upward. "Would you like me to help with the baby-sitting for a time? I'd love to. I'm bored silly at home as it is."

"Oh, would you? I'd feel so much better having you here." At the time, Ed was spending three hours on those days, working out of the house as an insurance salesman when I attended classes. He didn't like it much.

So Dottie helped me in exchange for my giving her twelve-year-old daughter, Tammy, piano lessons. When I announced my fourth pregnancy at the end of the second semester, Dottie howled at me for days.

"Four babies and four methods of birth control," I tried to joke.

My mother and I had now managed to establish a strained relationship of sorts. She was seeing the children on occasion and wanted to help pay Dottie for baby-sitting. I was grateful, to say the least.

Now a full-time student at Diablo Valley College, I found that first semester to be the toughest I had known. I'd expected it to me more difficult now that I had babies, compared to the days at University of Pacific when I was a music major and first met Ed. But I could not have guessed just how difficult. I was attending classes every day and studying all night much of the time.

"If you'd studied harder," my biology teacher said teasingly, "you wouldn't be having another baby so soon. More biology classes, that's what you need," she advised.

"What do you do," asked another teacher, "see how many units you can carry each time you're pregnant? Don't you think nineteen units is a bit excessive under the circumstances?"

"Facing piano students the minute I arrive home is the hard part," I told my husband. "Then, seeing my babies with their noses pressed against the sliding-glass doors, watching me spend time teaching piano to other people's children, that's rough, too."

"Once you earn your teaching credentials," he replied, "you'll be able to get a good job. And we'll be able to live better. Besides, you love teaching children, don't you?"

"Of course I do," I replied honestly. "They provide a creative outlet for me, and besides, I love them."

"Then stop complaining. *Our* kids will understand one day."

But when exhaustion set in, I often had to reevaluate things and wonder if it was really worth it.

Like most college students, I dreaded writing term papers. I rarely had fewer than three or four to write each semester, and their importance as far as grades were concerned made them cause overwhelming pressure. Although I liked the smell of coffee far better than the taste, I consumed great quantities of the stuff every night before examinations or when course papers were due. I could sometimes get by on two hours of sleep and often had no more than four, but after several nights of two to four hours of sleep, it showed in both my appearance and performance.

This was brought clearly into focus one afternoon when six-year-old Chris, my blond, blue-eyed cherub, came into the house with a blue-belly lizard some other child had given him. He looked up at my eyes with their dark half-moon hollows beneath them. I had never been so exhausted. Following my example of flipping creatures over to determine their sex—he had just seen me do this with kittens in a litter—he studied the lizard as it wisely played dead.

"Boy or girl?" he asked me, a puzzled look on his face.

"Gee, I'm not sure," I said, equally puzzled. "I think it's a girl."

He smiled up at me. "Good, 'cause I named it 'Mommy.' "

"Mommy?"

"Yeah." Chris giggled, " 'Cause she has eyes just like *you*."

Then he doubled over in giggling appreciation of his joke.

Exhausted as I was, I kept going, knowing that for me energy always surged when I set goals. I had learned that one could be swept beyond the desire to give up.

Dottie, surely my best friend in the world, kept me company. She would come over and chain-smoke as she watched me type, using the hunt-and-peck system. It was disconcerting to hear her chuckle as she watched me.

"Will you cut that out!" I'd finally spin around and confront her.

"I can't smoke when I laugh," she would tell me, aware that her smoking disturbed me. "Which do you think is better for my health?"

That always shut me up, so I put up with her good-natured derision—and her very welcome company and support.

I earned my Associate of Arts degree from Diablo Valley College and transferred to San Francisco State University, nearly forty miles from my home. At first, I often made the trip to the university twice a day, taking both morning and evening classes and sandwiching piano students into my afternoons. Putting my children to bed after their dinner and hurrying back across the bridge to school at night was arduous, but studying long hours after my 11 P.M. return was worse.

Dottie became a chronic "clucker," as I called her. She hovered over me to make sure I was taking care of myself, made snide comments about my husband at every opportunity, and fretted over my children, too. She was alone now. Her husband had a girl friend and he had moved out.

Her daughter, an only child, was living with her father. The divorce had been his idea, and Dottie was devastated without her child around.

"Tammy just wanted to live with her daddy," Dottie said. "His girl friend is young and pretty and fusses over her a lot. Maybe that's got something to do with it." So Dot lavished attention on my own brood.

I had only three semesters to go before earning my bachelor's degree. My marriage was also ending. I had filed for a divorce just before a visit to my doctor confirmed my worst fears.

"I saw your folder on my desk, and it's ruined my day," he said. He placed a paternal hand on my shoulder. "You might joke that you've had four children with four methods of birth control, Jann, but I have a hunch that deep down you really like having babies."

"That may be true, but I've just filed for divorce, and another mouth to feed is disastrous," I told him tearfully.

"Well, there's no doubt that you're pregnant again." He turned and stood staring out the large window of his office. I felt warmed by his concern for me and by his distress. I got up, slowly, said good-bye, and left the office.

Dottie had made an offer that I would have to consider. "Come with me to Tiajuana," she had suggested the day before, when I had told her about the pending doctor's visit. "I'll loan you the money, Babe."

"I can't even think about abortion," I told her. "That's the last thing I'd ever do."

"Don't think of it as having a baby," she admonished. "Think of it as losing something no larger than a peanut, certainly nothing you'd recognize as human."

"I can't help it. . . ."

But by the time I left my doctor's office, I felt closer to taking her up on her advice and help.

That night, after arrangements for our little "vacation" were made, I climbed up on a chair to retrieve an overnight case from a shelf in the closet. I slipped off the chair, and it toppled over on its side. As I fell, four baby books slid off the shelf, scattering their loose contents of birthday cards and photographs. I leaned against the chair and assessed the damage. Was my unborn baby hurt? was my first thought, accompanied by tears of regret and sorrow. The baby books of my other children lay beside me, and as I looked at the picture of Donice on her first day of kindergarten, Chris taking his first steps, Warner grinning toothlessly at a new stuffed toy, Rod pulling himself up in his playpen, I knew that I would have this fifth baby and love it as much as I did the others. Abortion was, for me, a mistake, and I could not go through with it.

I called Dottie and told her. "Well," she said softly, "you've probably made the only decision that's right for *you*. As for me, I would be headed for Tiajuana right now."

The birth of Marna LeAnne on Valentine's Day, 1964, was a high point, just as the other births had been. I was elated over this beautiful baby with her long dark hair and feminine little face.

At six weeks she came down with pneumonia and was hospitalized. My sense of helplessness was dreadful. I drove to the hospital every three to four hours around the clock to nurse her, trying to keep up the other schedules of school and home life as well.

Certain "tests" were casually suggested, but my optimistic nature overruled them and I took my coughing baby home without them. She never lost the cough, a cough that grew steadily worse. There were other signs that made this child different from her brothers and her sister, signs that worried me. I went along with the internist who checked her monthly, believing what he told me despite my suspicions, because he told me what I wanted to hear.

"Relax, Mama," he would say. "This tyke is going to grow up just like the others. Relax! You should be an old pro by now."

In 1965, when Marna had a second bout with pneumonia, the battery of tests I had previously turned down were given, and the diagnosis was cystic fibrosis. I remember fighting my way out of a crowded elevator in the hospital to stand heaving into my purse outside in the corridor because I couldn't find the restroom in time. I remember Ed's detachment when he heard the diagnosis, and my conviction that she was going to die and that it was somehow Divine retribution for my even considering abortion in the first place.

"That's crazy bullshit," Dottie said in her no-mincing-words authoritative way. "If you believe in God at all, you know it!"

Beautiful, intelligent little Marna was only a year old now. I wondered if she would live to see two.

"We can only manage this disorder, not cure it," the physician told me. "With the antibiotics available to us and aggressive physical therapy administered at home as often as needed, Marna has a chance of living a reasonably comfortable life."

"How . . . long?" The words seemed to have an unreal echo, as if they had been locked up in my throat.

He hesitated too long. "Most children born with this genetic disorder don't live into their teens, but"—he caught what must have been despair in my eyes—"we're seeing more and more all the time who do."

"Percentages?" I muttered.

"I can't give you percentages. Let's just say that Marna has an excellent chance of being around when a cure is found. Research is going on right now with that goal. It's possible for her to have a reasonably comfortable life."

There, he said it again: *"Reasonably* comfortable life!" The words made me sick to my stomach. They seemed like a cruelly deceptive euphemism for a life filled with illness and suffering, a life *almost* bearable.

"But many children do quite well on medication and therapy," he said. "Some are seldom hospitalized, and of course there are different degrees of the disorder, and milder cases . . ."

"Is Marna's a milder case?"

"Yes," he said, "I think so. The physical therapists here at the hospital will teach you how to give her therapy, and she'll have to take special medications to help her digestion. You'll have lots to learn. I've put a call through to the medical specialties company that furnishes the mist equipment for her bed, and . . ."

His words seemed to fade beyond my understanding. Stunned, I saw his lips move but could not comprehend what he was saying.

Three months to go before graduation and my degree, and suddenly all that I had worked for over several years did not count anymore. I missed classes, I couldn't concentrate on my studies, and the only thing that mattered was to be with my baby and hug her, cradle her, comfort her. If there had not been four other children at home, I gladly would have lived right there in the hospital, sleeping in the chair beside Marna's bed.

After I graduated from high school, I insisted on seeing the Semples and visited them often. They stood up for me at my wedding to Ed, which my parents refused to attend, and they had been my loving supporters ever since.

Peggy and Warner, now in their late seventies, visited me weekly after my marriage. When we learned of Marna's illness, Peggy spent hours holding Marna close, rocking her gently, as tears silently trickled down her face. "Oh, honey," she often said to me, "if only God would take me instead. I'm old and ready to go, but this beautiful baby . . . I just can't bear it."

"Peggy! Marna's going to make it. You'll see, she'll survive this thing!"

"I feel so helpless," Peggy wept. "There's nothing I can do to help you or the baby."

"You're here, and that's doing a great deal for me," I told her. "You have always been at my side when I needed you. Both of you. That's all I could ask."

It was different for Marna's father. I never knew if he was just innately detached or if he agreed with his own father's belief that there truly was a stigma attached to having a genetically imperfect child. I remember his statement after hearing about Marna: "Well, we still have four other healthy children." Perhaps he meant it to comfort me, but I heard in those words a chilling resignation and indifference. The more that was demanded of me in caring for her, the greater his invisibility. Finally, I made the break that had seemed inevitable for so long, freeing myself from the one commitment that seemed hopeless in order to concentrate more on those that might survive.

In April of 1965 there were three major turning points in my life. One was cause for celebration: I was on my way to earning a bachelor of arts degree. One triggered my sense of loss, failure, and anxiety: a pending divorce. And the third was the harbinger of my greatest sorrow:

Marna's illness, an illness that would eventually take her life.

Divorce had not been my husband's idea. He struggled against it the way a nonswimmer struggles in deep water. There was more pain than anger in his voice that warm April afternoon when he packed to leave forever. "You're selfish, depriving these kids of a father who loves them," he said. "And you're crazy if you think you'll ever find another man who'll want you with five kids, and one of them with cystic fibrosis!"

"What makes you think I'd be looking for another man?" I shot back. "I'll have my hands full as it is, without asking for more problems. Once I get a teaching job, the kids and I will get by!"

"You'll see how difficult it is without a man in your life, and once I'm gone, there will be no one else for *you!*" he shouted. I believed him, of course.

When he called in October 1965, to say he was leaving for Vietnam as a director with the USO, our divorce was only filed, not final. He hoped that during his absence I would have time to think things over and reconsider. "Perhaps you'll see how much you need me," he said. "You'll have the time to realize that you really love me, too."

Like millions of Americans in 1965, I regarded the war in Vietnam as a brief and sorrowful skirmish, a political strategy beyond my understanding, a war that couldn't last too long.

At that time I identified with the Hawks and idealistically believed that U.S. aid was essential if we were to prevent the threat of Communism from spreading. Assisting the valiant South Vietnamese in their civil war against the Communist-supported Viet Cong meant the conflict should be over without great losses. That's how naive I was.

At the time, I would have had trouble locating Vietnam on a map. I glanced at the newspaper headlines infrequently and followed the world news perfunctorily as I concentrated on my own little world which seemed on the verge of crumbling around me.

Although I had been the one to initiate the divorce, I still had a smothering sense of failure, intensified by a deep sense of loneliness that invariably struck after the children were tucked into bed at night.

My husband had been right about things being tough after he left, but at least most of the emotional stress our relationship generated was gone. The knowledge that he had *chosen* to travel with the USO to Vietnam mainly to see more of the world and have "the growth and development that travel can foster" gave me a false idea about what was going on in that country, particularly since I had also heard that Americans had things pretty soft over there.

Ed continued to importune me from Vietnam:

Think of the kids and don't do this to them and to me. In trying to go it alone, you are behaving selfishly and without thought for any of us. I'm sorry for all the things I did to hurt you. I'm not perfect. No one is. For all of us concerned, please just drop this silly divorce so we can go back to being a happy little family. . . .

Perhaps Donice would like a nice pen pal? Her name is Miss Diep Nguyen, and she works here at the library. She is 25 years old and has two baby girls. She is very anxious to know you, and will write shortly to Donice.

At no time did I ever consider a reconciliation. I knew that it took different sets of circumstances to make each of us "happy," and despite the strain and traumas I faced after Ed's departure, I was truly happier.

Although I leveled with him on this, his letters continued to be optimistic about our getting back together. When I remained unyielding on the subject, he finally wrote to tell me about the pretty Vietnamese girl he had met at a Christmas party shortly after his arrival, and he sent me her picture. It was the same Diep Nguyen he had mentioned in his earlier letter.

"The old jealousy tactic, huh?" Dottie snorted as she looked at the small black-and-white photo. "You're not going to cave in on this one, are you?" There was an edge to her voice.

"Of course not," I replied. "Our divorce is a long way from being final, but it's already past history in my mind."

"In his last letter he's begging for a reconciliation, and in this one he's showing you the competition. Nice!"

"Well, I'm numb to it all," I said as I plugged in Marna's suctioning machine.

"Where'd he meet her, anyhow?"

"Some Christmas party. She's a librarian with the USO, I think. The letter says she has two little girls. He wants her to be little Donice's pen pal. Can you believe it?"

Within two weeks, a letter dated March 17, 1966, came from the Vietnamese woman. The letter was—as Ed had promised—addressed to my ten-year-old daughter, Donice.

I decided not to show Donice the letter at that time and filed it away in an old shoe box, and it was soon forgotten. My thoughts at the time were to avoid any questions about Diep's and Ed's possible relationship, questions whose answers would have been only guesses, anyhow. It would be months before I looked at the March 17th letter again and wrote my first reply.

The day before I was to receive my degree in English from San Francisco State University, Marna woke with a high fever and congestion. My three-year-old Roddy had had a bad cold, and a bad cold for one of my other children could and often did lead to a much more serious problem for the baby. She had caught his cold, and even three separate therapy sessions with the suction machine were to little avail on this day.

Each time I admitted Marna to Children's Hospital I felt the old fear, the anguish at leaving her behind. Kindly nurses would attempt to distract her as I slipped out of the ward, but she was wise to them. I'd hear her sobbing in my dreams at night, feel a mixture of guilt and longing over leaving her in that dreaded place, and emotionally whip myself as I wondered if I could have prevented this latest episode of illness.

I walked up to receive my B.A. degree that June day in 1965 with my mother and beloved foster mother and foster father present, and of course four small children stood with them and cheered me on as well. With my Marna in the hospital, there was no time for the university reception afterward, and no special celebration. I went directly to her, the cap and gown lying on the car seat with my wonderful diploma. I was greeted by a very sick but smiling child and a poster—made by one of the nurses—that read: "My mama is a grad today. Congratulations!"

"You're finally through," one of the nurses said.

"No, not quite," I told her. "In order to teach on the college level, I still have a long way to go."

Dottie's husband, Randy, phoned her one June evening to say that he and his girl friend had broken up and asked if he and their daughter, Tammy, could "come home for a while." At first Dottie was angry and told him it was out of the question, but then she changed her mind. It had been several weeks since she had seen Tammy, and she

had to admit that she still loved Randy, "no matter what."
She called him back, and he and Tammy were on the next
plane.

"It was as if he'd never been gone," she gushed the
following weekend. "The whole miserable last six months
just don't exist anymore, and his girl friend did such a
number on him that I know he'll never see her again."

"You're taking him back? The divorce won't go
through?"

"Listen, Janni, there are . . . things . . . I've done in
our marriage that I'm not proud of, and things he's forgiven me for. Well, I love him and that's all that counts."
She grabbed at a kitchen towel and began swiping at the
plates draining in the dish rack.

"You don't have to dry my dishes." I took the towel
away from her and handed her a cup of coffee.

"You don't have any kind of life," Dottie said melo-
dramtically.

"Huh?"

"Look at you. Young, pretty, a lot to offer . . ."

"Five children! Now, what man could refuse such an
offer?" I went back to washing my dishes.

"Seriously . . ." Dottie began.

"Hey, friend, that *is* serious." I handed her the dish
towel. "Maybe you *should* wipe my dishes, after all. It
will put you back in touch with reality."

"Your old man's going out, so why shouldn't you? That
Vietnamese girl he's seeing . . . you know they're not just
playing Scrabble."

"I don't see how it makes any difference what he's do-
ing," I said. "By the time the kids are in bed at night and
I've finished Marna's therapy, I'm ready for bed myself.
Who has the time or energy for any social life?"

Marna began coughing in the next room. I turned to

listen, aware of Dottie's troubled frown as she watched me intently. "I just wish you'd have a little fun. At this pace, you won't hold up long enough to remember how," she told me.

Within two weeks following my graduation, I applied for graduate school and enrolled in a summer program. It was in one of my classes that I met Joe. About thirty years old, he was a good-looking assistant professor at San Francisco State University. With him I found myself beginning to experiment with flirting once again. I guess I had reached a point of vulnerability without realizing it; being the accomplished and experienced seducer that he was, Joe recognized it at once.

He was always polite. Whenever we ran into each other following one of my evening classes he would look soulfully into my eyes as he asked how I was. I wanted to believe that he cared. It had been a long time since a man seemed genuinely concerned about me, and his attention was flattering.

One evening he stopped me as I was leaving my graduate seminar classroom. His gaze was kind and appreciative.

"Do you have time for coffee?" he asked seductively; one could substitute almost any kind of invitation in place of the word "coffee."

"I have a baby-sitter, but I've got to be home by eleven."

"You're not wearing your wedding ring anymore," he observed in a soft, modulated baritone. "I always notice when a woman is as lovely as you." (*That* should have been my warning. Instead, I craved more.)

"Let's go in my car," he said soothingly, baiting the hook.

Together we walked silently toward the parking lot, each of us probably considering all the possibilities that could result from having a simple cup of coffee. Joe was a toucher. When he talked, every word had its own particular kind of emphasis, punctuated by a pat on my arm or my hand. Enthusiasm was demonstrated by a squeeze of my arm, and a little joke was accented by a tap on my nose or chin.

I don't remember the restaurant or the coffee.

Of course, neither of us wanted to end the evening afterward. Our initial talk of commonplaces became conversation of a more serious nature. The long looks accompanied by long silences both thrilled and scared me. What was I allowing here? But I savored it all as I invited more.

After driving around the campus for a while, Joe suddenly pulled over and parked, then whispered seductively, "The very first time I ever saw you, I said to myself, 'Gorgeous! I have to know her!' " His voice was husky now.

"You had such a wistful look," he continued. "That expression, like someone who has been terribly hurt . . ." The inflection of the last word was raised, an implicit question mark to elicit my confirmation and heart-rending story. I did not comply.

"Our love affair will set off the next San Francisco earthquake," he boasted, pulling me to him. I slipped off my shoes, curled up in his arms as he whispered hoarsely in my ear:

"There's one thing, before we start this, which you must know. I have a wife and three kids whom I love and will never leave. I demand absolute honesty in my relationships. I believe in having total honesty with my women right up front."

"This honesty—does your wife know that you . . ."

"Of course not. It'd kill her."

I looked at my watch in the light of an oncoming car's headlights and quickly slipped into my shoes, wondering how long it would be before I took Dottie's advice again.

Not long after I had called a halt to Joe, Dottie went to work for an Oakland law firm and had to give up baby-sitting for me.

Another friend, a soft-spoken woman who had cared for my children in the past and whom I trusted completely, took over the baby-sitting while I took graduate classes at San Francisco State University.

"You've got to keep up your strength so you can handle all the demands made on you," she said solicitously one morning as I gathered my books together and looked for my car keys. Then Marna coughed in that deep, spasmodic, throat-searing way that I knew I would never become used to.

I had quickly plugged in the suctioning machine and attached the catheter when Dottie walked in without knocking, which was her habit. "My boss is ill today," she explained, "and the other guys said I'd caught them up enough and could have the day off. . . . Say, aren't you going to be late for class?" She looked at me with alarm.

I already had Marna head down on my stretched-out legs and was cupping my hand in position over her lungs. "This comes first," I said.

"I'd help if I had the stomach for it, but I can't watch this," Dottie said under her breath.

Marna's dark eyes widened when she saw the suctioning equipment on the kitchen table. We went through this procedure at least twice daily, but it was a battle every time. The pitiful screaming began even before I had her in position for her therapy treatment; there were sixteen different positions on a slant board, "cupping" and "vibrating" the palm of my hand over her tiny body. The suctioning was the worst part, of course. When she fought the catheter, her face turned purple, her eyes bugged, and sometimes she was able to bring the end of the rubber catheter over her tongue and out her mouth, preventing it from traveling into her trachea.

Dottie sat in the next room. I could see the smoke from her cigarette circling the back of the couch. As I suctioned, Marna gasped, gagged, and yelled. Dottie finally got up and went outside, shutting the door behind her noisily.

Cuddling time followed the treatment as I held the warm, wet-cheeked infant close and crooned a lullaby. She immediately quieted, but when I put her down in her crib and heard her last convulsive sobs fade into sleep, I put my head against the bars of her crib and wept uncontrollably.

A hand came to rest on my shoulder. Dottie had returned, her own face streaked with tears.

"I'm here for you, kid," she said in a husky voice.

Later, as we had coffee at the kitchen table, I showed her a letter from my ex-husband. Letters from him came frequently to the children and to me. He seemed to be enjoying his stay in Da Nang. According to the newspaper accounts, the total strength of U.S. forces by the end of 1965 was over 181,000, but Da Nang apparently had been relatively quiet. In any case, Ed never mentioned the war.

"How does he like Vietnam?" Dottie asked sarcastically.

I shrugged. "Apparently very much. He still writes letters pleading for a reconciliation, though."

"You can't make it on piano-lesson money."

"I don't know, Dottie. I can't find a teaching job without teaching credentials, although I *might* be hired at some school district if they desperately needed a teacher. I understand that in such a case, the school can apply for my credentials."

"The trick is to find some district that doesn't have twenty English teachers for every job!" she said glumly. "What you need is a rich boyfriend."

"Come on! What would I do with him! I hardly have time for . . ."

"Somewhere between wiping noses and other things, there must be time for a man in your life, Jann!"

"A man is the last thing I want to clutter up my life right now," I said emphatically. "First, I must get a job and heal the scars from the last ten years. That might take lots of time."

One July afternoon in 1965 I answered the door to find a tall, pleasant-looking man who introduced himself as Larry Jansen, an insurance and securities salesman. It was a scorchingly hot summer day, and my street just happened to be the shadiest, he said. Besides, this was the first time he had ever tried prospecting door to door.

I told him politely that I was the single parent of five children and could not afford securities or insurance. He made a face and asked me if I knew how many children I had over the national average. Although he did not realize it, that was not a good beginning.

We made polite conversation, and when he left, I noticed he had a funny-looking little yellow car. I paid scant attention to cars in those days, but I was later to learn that he drove a Porsche, his one and only possession of any value. On our next meeting, about two months later, he began to give me an education about automobiles, in response to my referring to his Porsche as "that funny-looking little car."

During those two months I had turned him down when he called to ask me out to dinner. Then one September night I gave in and we went out, in spite of frowns and puzzled expressions of my children. I felt a little giddy, like a teenager on her first date, and worried that I'd made a wrong decision. The children had not made it any easier, either.

After this date, there were several evening visits to my home, followed by all-night phone calls; we talked about ourselves—our philosophies, dreams, tastes, our beliefs from religion to politics. One evening Larry announced: "I like children—after all, I have two from my first marriage—but even so I never felt any great need to be a father." We sat in lawn chairs in the garden, enjoying the balmy September weather. A full moon lit the entire yard with that pale blue light that casts an eerie, unreal glow that allows one to see everything. I had a dreamy sense that nothing happening was real, that the romantic connection I experienced with this man was imaginary.

He took my hand and drew me into the lawn chair with him. We snuggled silently for a long time, neither of us wanting to break the spell. I knew that we were on the verge of serious considerations, and my heart beat faster in anticipation.

"I'd marry you in a minute," he said at last. "I just don't know about all those kids."

"I certainly can understand." It had all happened too quickly, within a week and a half of our first date. I fought the dizziness caused by his words and my feelings.

"I love the two kids from my first marriage, but taking on that brood of yours! I just don't know." He lit a cigarette and leaned back in the chair. I put my head on his chest sadly. How could I blame him? Giving up his freedom for a woman with five children was insanity, and already some of his friends—aware that he was in love with me—were offering advice in an attempt to "save" him from a terrible mistake.

"On the other hand," he said at last, "I've grown awfully fond of those little rascals. And I know I don't want to live without you. I don't know what kind of a provider I'll be, but I do want to marry you, Jann. Would you consider it?"

The proposal came just twelve days after our first evening together!

Larry came by almost every evening after that. Most of our courting took place in my living room with all five children present. He and I spent hours and hours just talking, arguing, talking. He saw the house when everything was wrong with it, including the time I accidentally flushed a dirty diaper down the toilet and flooded the hallway! He saw dishes stacked for two days in the sink, my children when they were at their brattiest, me when I was my crabbiest. And still he wanted to marry me.

During the months before we married, Larry and I had some major adjustment difficulties. One of our problems concerned Larry's admitted struggle with his pending loss of freedom and his anxiety at being tied down to a big family. My defensiveness each time this topic came up was no help. Larry was honest with me: five children were enough of a burden, but he also admitted his reservations about being able to handle the "sick child situation," too, and despite the fact that I truly understood how he felt, I was still hurt each time we discussed it.

For my part, with five children, two dogs, and three cats, it was impossible for me to maintain a glossy image for long. Too many demands kept me moving, although friends often complimented me, saying that I never appeared frazzled. If they could only have known the pressure and effort it took for me to keep up that easygoing, serene appearance! With Marna's daily therapy and care, money problems, classes (still), and piano students, to say nothing about caring for my four other lively children and my homework studies, I was never still.

I usually planned Marna's therapy sessions before her meals so that she could enjoy eating with less congestion, and I always planned her therapy before I expected Larry to drop by. One afternoon, however, she was particularly congested and I decided to suction her.

Fear and anger and screaming protests always accompanied her violent struggling as I worked over her. This twenty-month-old baby cried and fought with tremendous determination when she faced her therapy. She had learned by now how to deftly pull the catheter out of her mouth with her monkeylike toes. This time, there was the usual gurgling and hold-the-breath routines that I had witnessed daily yet never failed to find frightening.

Eyes bugged, Marna began turning purple as she tried to bite my hand in her frenzy to keep me from reinserting the catheter.

"Marni, Marimouse," I crooned to her, "I *have* to do this. I'm so sorry, sweetheart, but I have to . . ."

Her lovely eyes became panicky once again as she felt the slippery catheter move down through her nostril into her trachea, and she tried to maneuver to block its passage with her tongue. As I held her tightly, close to my body, and flipped on the suctioning device with my elbow, I felt sudden gratitude that she possessed the strength to fight me.

When it was over, we cuddled and wept together. "This

is one battle I *must* win for both of us,'' I told her. ''Then one day, you'll win the major one.''

Holding Marna close, I could feel the vibrations of loosened congestion rattling inside her chest. There was only one thing to do for her.

''I have to work harder on those slant positions, love,'' I told her. She seemed to know exactly what was coming. I hugged her lovingly, trying to reassure her, and when I set up the slant board once again, she whimpered with exhaustion. My arms and back ached, too, and I was grateful that she was too tired to put up the same fight this time.

As was often the case, nosebleeds followed the catheter suctioning, and this afternoon both of us were covered with blood. When I again placed the catheter down her nose I wondered at her sudden calm. There was a stillness in her eyes, and then she actually started to smile as she gazed intently over my shoulder.

I turned to look behind me and there was Larry, shock in his eyes as he saw my bloody hands and Marna's bloody little face. He leaned against the door frame, and seeing the expression in his eyes, I thought, ''Oh, no. It's the end for us.''

He quickly recovered as our eyes met, but he was still unsmiling. I waited for him to turn and leave, waving me off. I waited for him to tactfully explain how this was more than he had bargained for. With pounding heart, I anticipated the dreadful hurt to come.

During that long silence I mentally tried to come up with a brave reply to what I knew he would have to say. I prayed that I would not cry until after he had gone.

Larry leaned over Marna as if to say good-bye and spoke to her soothingly as he stroked her head. Then he turned to me and said, "All right, honey. Show me how I can help."

We were married on July 4, 1966. Ironically, it was Larry who had chosen Independence Day for our wedding date—the same Larry who bought a year's supply of shoe-laces for the children at a Payless sale, who helped them with their homework, who tucked them in at night, who assisted in giving Marna's therapy.

My "adopted parents," Peggy and Warner, then in their late seventies, and a couple with whom Larry worked joined Velma, an old friend, and Dottie and her neighbors at our simple ceremony. Of course there were the five children, full of giggles and happiness as they sat huddled together, grinning in the front row of the stark church sanctuary. ("This will be a gym or recreation room when we can afford to build the real sanctuary," the pastor had told us.)

There was neither music nor flowers, other than the cor-sages the women wore. The entire exchange of vows took only ten minutes, making it hard to believe that Larry and I had made such a great commitment that morning. Larry, in his dark blue suit, and I, in my beige lace dress with matching hat, were still in the rhythm that had preceded this event. The morning had been frenetic, trying to dress five lively children, find clean socks, re-iron wrinkled shirts that had been neatly pressed prior to being put on the first time, play referee for sibling battles over who really spilled the orange juice or grabbed the last pancake.

Peggy Semple was to baby-sit during the four days we planned to honeymoon. As competent as Peggy was, I was still anxious when I saw how congested Marna was that day. Much as I dreaded starting our new marriage by can-

celing our honeymoon trip, leaving a child who might be
coming down with a serious infection was unthinkable.

"Look, darling, if you call each night I'll tell you exactly how the baby is doing, and I'll take her to the hospital right away if it seems warranted," Peggy assured
me.

Larry and I left for a trip up the coast, staying at a motel
the first night and camping the other three. When we returned, we made a sad trip to the hospital with Marna.

"Now, I don't want you going through that guilty-
mother routine," Peggy warned me after we returned from
having our baby admitted. "You'll always have to weigh
and balance things when you have such a sick baby. Sometimes one of the other children might need you more than
Marna, and sometimes it will be your husband. It will
drive you crazy at times, trying to keep the balance, but I
know you can do it, sweetheart."

I looked at Larry. Marna was in good hands right now,
and at this particular moment my husband needed me
more. I'd go to the hospital later that evening with a special toy for her and an hour or more of cuddling. Right
now I knew Larry needed his wife, and I took his hand.

Just two months after Larry and I were married, I was
hospitalized for an operation that we had expected would
be routine but was not. Severe complications kept me hospitalized for three weeks, and I needed to return to the
hospital intermittently for four months afterward.

Being a father to five children without a wife at home
had not been part of our bargain, and much of the time I
found Larry exhausted and miserable. His work suffered,
and our financial situation went from bad to critical. On
top of this, he was trying to quit smoking.

"Never try to quit smoking when your life is in upheaval,'' a friend advised him, but Marna's lung problem and some unpleasant symptoms of his own, which Larry attributed directly to his smoking, made him want to quit just the same.

Since I had never smoked—apart from playing around with cigarettes in high school—I had no idea just how traumatic stopping could be for people truly addicted to nicotine. I can't count the number of times Larry had to climb up on the roof late at night to retrieve his ''last pack,'' or how many times he snapped and snarled when actually the only trouble was that he was experiencing withdrawal symptoms.

One Sunday morning following my return from one of my hospitalizations, Chris and his brother Warner got into a noisy battle. Larry investigated and, deciding that Chris was at fault, promptly paddled him. It was not a harsh or serious spanking, but the next thing I knew, Larry came into our bedroom where I was lying in bed, sat down on the floor with his back to the closed door, and began to weep. It was then that I fully realized how much pressure he had been under.

Not long after my hospitalization, I woke to my former
husband telling me about his latest business

Chapter Two

Diep

Not long after my hospitalization, I wrote to my former husband to tell him about my remarriage. I received another letter from his pretty Vietnamese girlfriend, Diep. I looked in my closet for the shoebox containing her first letter and read it over, closely examining the neat handwriting and the accompanying photo of the demure and lovely young woman.

The writer of that letter, Nguyen Thi Diep, was born in the Bac Ninh province of North Vietnam. As she told it, her father, Ho Nguyen, was "a smart man who worked for a French banker in Hanoi and knew how to speak the French language." Concerned that Communism was gaining power in the North, her father decided to bring his family to Saigon when Diep was in her early teens.

After arriving in Saigon, Ho was hired as a military policeman by the South Vietnamese government. Diep's mother, Vu Thi Kim, was a strong influence on her. She described her as "a warm, gentle lady with high standards, of high class and culture. She not say much ever, but was very quiet and wise."

When the youngest of Vu Thi Kim's nine children was born, she learned that her husband was keeping a mistress in town who had had two children by him. Vu kept silent, holding in her grief when her husband decided to stay with the other woman. She never spoke of her suffering to her children, so when she gradually began to fade, becoming weaker and weaker, no one realized that she was actually dying from grief.

When Vu Thi Kim died, suddenly and unexpectedly, Diep, the eldest child, was in her first year of college; the youngest was only sixteen months old.

Ho Nguyen was filled with grief and remorse. He suffered from high blood pressure and soon found himself unable to work. Since there was no son to take over, Diep quit college and went to work. Eleven people, including her father and his mistress, were dependent on her paycheck.

As she later told me: "In Vietnam, I was pretty, popular, a good student and quite innocent when I first attended college. Before that, I knew Catholic schools in early grades. I had high ideals, and I had a family of little brothers and sisters who were like my own babies from the beginning. I feel sad looking back on those days, days with their innocence and with the happy, carefree, easy life that I led. I was raised in a family which followed Confucius. I attended Catholic high school, and went to college in 1962–63. That was the dawn of my beautiful time.

"I fell in love that first year of college with a Vietnamese man whom I had known since childhood and met again in college. Like me, he was from North Vietnam originally. When we were children, we had attended the same Catholic schools. He was Catholic, and I was not.

"Our love was innocent. Studying and knowledge were our mutual loves as well. We held education to be all important. I loved him so much. He was my first real love.

"When my mother died that same year, there was no son in the family to take over the care of our family. Our family's survival was up to me. But something unexpected happened! My sweetheart's love for me cooled when I left college. He said that without higher education, I would be lower station than he in life, and so I lost both my mother and my lover at the same time. It broke my heart.

"I went to study English night time and worked as cashier for the USO club in Da Nang, later worked as a hostess at the officers' club and then at the USO library for the U.S. Army.

"I liked the American men I met at the USO. I often felt such sympathy for them when they were homesick and lonely. I was lonely, too, for my lost love.

"It was after the World War II that there were many books written against the old ways and customs, beliefs and traditions. The Western customs and ideas crept into Vietnam, and I liked the Western ideas and living, finding myself between the old ways of Vietnamese culture and the Westerners' new ideas. I felt like deserter, sometimes, as between the Catholic and Buddhist, but I believed in God, I knew."

As she studied magazines from America, poring over pictures of what was obviously a more comfortable lifestyle and admiring the beautiful, serene-looking men and women who posed for ads that intrigued her, Diep identified more and more with American culture.

Then she met a handsome young army major. Their romantic involvement was immediate, and her family and friends scorned her: "They said I was modern girl of the new generation, that there were many modern Vietnamese girls working the bars, and they also had the American boyfriends in 1963, but they 'loved for money' and I loved for love. There were also the half-American children, and Vietnamese customs hated their mothers and did scorn them, too. They said they were prostitutes. I rejected that."

But Diep could not banish the stigma from her mind. She knew that the customs of her country would not condone her having an American lover. At first, she believed that in time her choice would be acceptable, especially when she found she was pregnant. The army major was unwilling to be responsible for this baby, however, and for the second time Diep found herself abandoned by a man. Fortunately, her family stood by her, accepting the baby daughter she brought into the world and accepting Diep as well.

"I really did not know anything when he and I first met. He took away my pure heart, my innocent soul, and then he went away without caring that I was with baby. Our relationship was short and I had been so innocent. I knew then how other Vietnamese girls felt all around me who were in the same situation as I was. I knew how it felt to be left."

A classic story, Diep's tale was the cliché of women during wartime. Her child, Jeanne (Mai-Cat), was born December 7, 1964, a dearly loved and wanted baby born to a young mother who was still rearing eight brothers and sisters, the youngest of whom was only two years older than her new baby.

When her baby was about a year old, Diep met another American army officer, a graduate of West Point who was a captain at the time. He treated her with respect and kindness, and in his gentle way he tried to teach her English so that they could communicate more easily. Their romance culminated in Diep's becoming pregnant for the second time, but this time she was truly in love with her baby's father. As she told me:

"We would write notes to each other, me with the help of Vietnamese/English dictionary in hand. Yes, I loved him. Once more I defied conventions of my people. My flaw: I was just a romantic girl.

"I feared the scorn of my friends and family. I also feared that my children would pay the bitter price of being American. I bleached my hair to light brown to look like the American girl, and it had been very black and long before. Now I wore it short in American style, like the American women whose pictures I had seen in magazines in the library.

"When I became pregnant with second baby, I was once again hurt by my people, so I rejected them back. But she was born, and I was proud of my cute, smart children. I had no thought of marrying my second baby's father at the time, but I still wanted to come to America where I knew my children would be accepted. My worry was over my younger brothers and sisters who needed my help and support, and my aging father needed me, too. What to do? I believed that my second baby's father might send for me then when he had to return to the States. Oh, I don't know what I really thought. I was so confused.

"Soon after Jolie, my second baby, was born, her daddy had to return to the United States. He had wanted me to go with him, but I couldn't leave my family there in Vietnam. I was still helping them, supporting them. There was nothing I could do, and he was of high rank then, lt. colonel by now, and his family at home would not have approved.

"I was just a Vietnamese girl who had passed him in life. But when he returned to the U.S., my heart was broken in two. He and I said good-bye with streaming tears from our eyes, knowing it would be a very long time before we would ever see each other again.

"I fell into a deep depression when he left. I didn't want to eat or anything. I wrote him many letters, and he did not answer. My depression grew worse and worse, making me very ill."

When Diep was introduced to the new USO director, her friends warned her not to go out with him. Diep worked at the army library, so she attended many USO parties, and it was at a Christmas party that her relationship with my husband began.

For weeks and weeks she had waited for some word from Jolie's father in the United States, but nothing came. Her rejection by Jolie's father made Ed's attention all the more welcome.

"He's not your kind. Forget him," her friends advised. When they saw Ed stop by her desk to inquire about some magazine or book, they gave her the same advice. "Stay away from him. Ignore him! He's not worth your time."

One evening one of the men stopped by her desk to talk. "The USO director likes you," he told her. "He's having a hard time getting over his split-up, and the two of you could comfort each other. After all, you're both lonely people."

As Diep told me:

"I wondered how he could be so lonely, taking out Vietnamese girls every night. He seemed nice, and he seemed so sad. I felt sorry for him.

"My children were very little, very cute and sweet. He seemed to like them, and that made me happy. I was lonely and bitter, and still waited for the letters that never came. When your former husband paid me attention, it was to make my hurt go away for a time.

"When I met your ex-husband, the war in my homeland had brought death to the Americans and Vietnamese and wasn't just in the country anymore. I worked still at the USO library, fearing the sounds of the jet planes and helicopters and the rockets, because they meant death. I was so sad and hurt as I brought my two babies to the library and hid them while I worked. My superiors would frown to see a mother bring her children on the job, so I made my good little girls keep very quiet as they slept and played while I worked in the library.

"When your husband appeared to me during that dark time and I was so hurt and sad, he told me: 'I am hurt same as you.' I told him my heart was cut in thousand pieces. He said he was crazy with pain, that he had lost you, his wife, whom he loved very much.

"He said you had divorced him, but he had hopes that you change your mind. Well, my soul was one half missing, too, and I had pity on him. Maybe I could make him happy, and he could make me peaceful in my heart. I had not heard from the man I loved for so long, and thought maybe I not hear from him ever again.

"By now, my family had accepted the Western culture

more. They loved my children and took care of them when I had to work. My children were my sisters' dolls.

"When one of my sisters worked at the officers' club, she fell in love with a lieutenant. Once I found them together. She was innocent and just eighteen. When I saw her later in his jeep, she left and didn't come home. He drove her all around and around each evening, and she was so afraid of us that we couldn't find her in Da Nang. He had finally taken her to Saigon.

"We were all very sad and depressed. Six months later I saw him and talked to him. I asked him where he keep my sister. Then he brought my sister back, and she was soon to have a baby boy. My family was not too happy to have three American babies in one family. But my brothers and sisters, they still loved them very much.

"Although I still wanted to be with Jolie's daddy very much, I allowed my romantic soul to go with your former husband. At first we just comfort each other about our pain.

"He helped me and I helped him, wanting all along to make some hope for my children. Perhaps he would help me get to the United States where it was safe, where my children would be accepted and where they would have a future. This is what I hoped.

"The war was closer now, and by January of 1967, Da Nang was calm by day and filled with fear by night."

The American military presence had increased to 486,000 men. At home the news showed unspeakable horrors, yet my former husband never mentioned anything at all. That he did not gave me a false sense of optimism, in spite of the news reports about Vietnam.

As early as May 1966, a report in *Time* said that ". . . the Administration's oft-stated position is quite clear.

If Hanoi really wants the U.S. to ground its bombers, it need only make some move toward de-escalation in return. Until it does, as the President put it before 100 farm leaders last week, 'all the king's horses and all the king's men are not going to move us out of our position.' ''

According to Diep, her life at the library at that time was peaceful. The library was housed in a portable Quonset building, small but certainly adequate for the several hundred books and magazines it held. There were two desks, and their name plaques on each desk gave the librarians a sense of status. Boxes of old magazines were stacked in the back of the building, which was unbearably hot much of the time. Two large circulating fans kept the librarians and military browsers reasonably comfortable but also compelled everyone to find weights to hold down loose papers.

Since no military building in Da Nang was considered permanent, everything was kept as simple as possible. A small kitchen was set up next to the main room, which served as the library, and its walls were covered with pictures of lovely young Vietnamese girls and American movie actresses.

In our talks after she came to this country, Diep told me about her job there.

''I was to work in several different places as librarian for American USO, and this was just one example. In morning I bring my little girls in bicycle basket and keep them on blankets beneath my desk to play and sleep during day. They keep very quiet. It was about five miles from my home near the river to military base, and the ride along the river each morning was pleasant and quiet.

''When the war come to Da Nang and there was shooting even during daytime, I have to watch very carefully to make sure no one hide near river and I get caught in gunfire. Until 1970 or 1971 it was not so dangerous, but after that I was often very scared.

"In those days I wore my *ao-dai* [traditional Vietnamese dress] most times. The Western dress did not look good on me, and the soldiers like to see the Vietnamese girls in their own dress. We fixed tea for soldiers during the monsoon season when it was colder and pouring rain outside, but most times they like Coke and 7-Up and beer.

"Parties were held every weekend, and all pretty Vietnamese girls went to them, usually with some soldier. I often went alone, but usually when I was not teaching Vietnamese at evening school or helping Vietnamese learn a little French or English there, I was home with my little girls.

"Your ex-husband, he came to me and ask if I like to write his little girl, Donice. I say that would be nice, but how about Mrs. Jannice? What would she think and say? He tell me that you were giving him the divorce, and that you would not mind, and he say that maybe I ask you what makes him happy, because you had made him so happy when you were married.

"Well, I sit down and write your daughter, worried that it make you unpleasant, but he say that it would not make you angry."

So Diep's first letter came, dated March 17, 1966, and addressed to my daughter Donice.

Dear Little Friend Donice,

I hope your mother will explain about me and your daddy with you. I don't know about the future, but I hope and wish one day I'll be lucky to see your country and you. I'll see the beauty of your country, and I'll tell you much about my country, too.

. . . Your daddy sent you something from his trip to Tokyo. He did? I have to remind him always, Donice. You give me your measurables and I'll send you a nice Vietnamese dress, like the young girls wear here, for your birthday. I think American clothes are not nice for Vietnamese . . . wear Vietnamese and Chinese dress, look better. I'll write you sometime about the flowers in Vietnam.

From Vietnam, with love,
Diep

Diep's allusions to Ed at the time confirmed my sense that she was more than just "a friend," and while it would pass over Donice's head, I decided to keep the information to myself and stashed the letter away.

Chapter Three

A Beginning
Correspondence
and Friendship

Diep's next letter to Donice was more impersonal, as if she sensed she had said too much before.

April 1966

Dear Little Friend,

Maybe my English is still poor. In Vietnam they are learning English much more than before. We learn two languages at high school, English and French. Most Vietnamese now they learn at "Vietnamese-American Association Centre Culture." They learn night time. The service men they help to improve their English. I'm lazy to learn, but every year I have to pass an examination about language.

Oh, I'm sending you some pictures to show about my country. Vietnam is small country in the world. Most people only know or hear about Vietnam from the war. Maybe the Third War will be in my country. Think of

me as your friend. Say hello to your brothers and sisters
and good regards to your mother. I close here.

From Vietnam, with love,

Diep

The letters that followed—sometimes addressed to Donice, sometimes to all the children—gave a picture of Diep's
country and her life there.

Dear Little Friends,

I hope your daddy showed my pictures to you and
your mother, and I hope this letter comes to you cheer-
fully. I wrote one letter to your mother. Your daddy
come back to home soon, he told me. You'll see.

I have two children. One is 3 years old and the other
is 1½ year old. They are the girls. I like children very
much. (We count one year ahead like Chinese.)

I wish to write your mother very much, but I am
afraid to make her unpleasant. I hope we will have a
friendly, and that she will understand me and write to
me often. I will answer you and tell you about my country. It is so beautiful without the war.

Your daddy say you are too young for me to write,
and he hope your mother will explain about us with you.
I pray God bless your daddy and me to be together in
the life, and I hope to make him happy. I am sending
you another picture with the affection and hope your
mother will let you have it. I like to have your picture
too. Say my good regards to her. I hope my late letter
not displease her.

Despite the openness of the appeal, Donice was only
mildly interested. As a country, Vietnam had no meaning
for her, and her father's new friend was simply that—a
friend. I, however, understood that Diep was more im-

portant to him than that and assumed that she might be
returning to the States with him one day.

Dear Donice,
    You like Vietnamese dress I make for you? It called
ao dai. I love my work. I make friendly with the books
in library where I work.
    My country is poor from the war. Eighty years belong
to French government. That is why Vietnamese understand French language. Now the war is civil one between North and South, and Viet Cong destroy many
people. People are hungry, but we are O.K. this time in
the war. The town is better than country.

I began to keep notes about the war. Diep's letters
sparked my interest in that tiny country's problems, making it all suddenly more interesting and important to me.
I often clipped articles, photographs, and news items from
various periodicals about the situation in Da Nang and
took greater interest in the evening TV news as well.
    An article from *Time Magazine* gave me some under-
standing of Diep's city:

    . . . Aside from scattered children playing and citi-
    zens shopping quietly, the Da Nang streets are strangely
    still in anticipation. The muffled explosions and popping
    sounds from distant warfare have become background
    music to their ears.

I read how greedy, parasitic businessmen from many
countries—not just the United States—were taking advantage of the sad conditions in Vietnam. It was a poor country struggling through a civil war while America's youth
disembarked from transport ships and planes like so many

toy soldiers off an assembly line. Unspeakable horrors, suffering, sickness, misery, death, corruption, and drugs— all were a part of the Vietnam of that time.

In the midst of this was Diep—and thousands like her— sitting in her little house with her children playing around her as she pressed Vietnamese wildflowers in a handmade card to send to us. I couldn't connect the images—they seemed too incompatible. To date, Diep's letters had portrayed a country more inconvenienced by war than dying from it. There was a wistful quality about her letters, a sadness when she mentioned the war, but their tone was generally romantic, optimistic, and light-hearted.

Dear Little Friend,

Your daddy and I love each other. I do not know what will be, but hope we be friends and would like writing your mother, but am afraid to make her unpleasant.

In the country they have the war and get killed more. In town, many people have TV, tape recorder and radio. In city, 15% of ladies wear Western clothes and attend French school. We attend French school and also learn the English.

I have to put down my pen now. I hope we get blessed to see each other one day, and that I çan spend the life with your daddy.

Say good regards to your mother and stepdaddy for me.

Diep

Diep, I thought, would probably want a friendly reception if she ever arrived in the States. I would give her that. I had no reason to be unfriendly to her, but I thought it inappropriate for me to correspond with her. My daughter also seemed disinclined to write to her, although I insisted she send a thank-you note when two lovely Vietnamese dresses arrived, one for Donice and a tiny one for Marna. I also wrote to Diep myself to thank her. It was obvious the dresses were handmade, and beautifully so.

Dear Diep,

Thank you very much for the Vietnamese dresses you made for my girls. I am not handy with a needle and thread, and so I appreciate such talent. Marni and Donice look so darling in the dresses, and I will send you a photo of them dressed up in the *ao dai* so you can see for yourself how nice they are.

Marni was just released from the hospital, where she has been admitted seven times during her young life. She is the same age as your older daughter. In fact, they are just a few months apart. You have undoubtedly heard about her illness. Well, she looks so much better, and her coloring is excellent. She was so happy to get home and see the lovely dress that came all the way from Vietnam for her. Thank you again.

Sincerely,
Jann Jansen

By now, I had filled my first journal with letters and clippings. This picturesque description of Vietnam lay taped beside one of Diep's letters to Donice.

American freighters queue up along a crescent of the muddy river, waiting for the undersize stevedores to transfer their cargoes to the American trucks choking the dockside streets.

In the inching downtown traffic, coolies haul handcarts between the bulging gasoline trucks with their ESSO and CALTEX emblems; pretty girls in flowing *ao dais* are honked aside by American pickup trucks. . . .

The sweltering heat rings with the noise of new apartments being built for Americans.

New stories described Saigon as a boom town for American businessmen. Never before, we were told, had our businessmen followed the troops to war on such a scale. Working as foremen, agents, and bosses, more than 2,000 U.S. civilians had poured into South Vietnam, building plants and roads and airstrips. They sold the troops everything from machetes to mutual funds, supposedly "propping up the tiny nation's war-torn economy." The contrast between the country's sorry state and this false sense of affluence confused and angered me.

My bewilderment grew, as surrealistic images of fierce jungle fighting appeared on the TV screen night after night. The Viet Cong looted, slashed, and burned through peasant homes; they traveled (we were told) among our soldiers as benign Vietnamese civilians during daylight hours and then returned again to their murderous activities after dark.

A clipping from *Newsweek* delineated the confusion:

Hanoi has been insisting that our U.S. air raids have been consistently killing civilians, to the Administration's denial. It turns out that American bombs are, after all, taking their toll on innocent civilians.

My scribbled notation followed the magazine's quote:

There were pictures on the news tonight of Hanoi schoolgirls digging shelters. . . .

In contrast to this, a letter from my ex-husband, Ed, made it seem that his life, at least, was untouched by the war:

Dearest Jann,

. . . Slated in the near future is, I think, my trip to
Australia. By the time I return to see you and our dear
children, I might have traveled to nearly every country
in the world. Think of that. I have souvenirs from my
travels for the children, so they will know their daddy
has succeeded in one of his life's dreams, to travel to
every country there is. Watch the mail for rings for each
of the children.

My love forever,
Ed

Ed made no mention of Diep, yet her letters were often
centered on him.

Dear Donice,

I'm happy that you and your mother liked the things
your daddy and I got in Da Nang town. I hope and pray
God bless us and let me be in your daddy's life. Both
we love together and he needs me. Your daddy is much
different than the first time he be here. He found happy
again in his life. I want to make him happy. Maybe I
learn something from your mother. She will tell me
something he like.

Da Nang is holding the summer sound. They sell all
kinds of flowers. Very nice. If my country is over the
war, how nice it is! You are very lucky to live in free
world and not having the war.

I hope God bless me to see your family and country
one day. The other ladies here they tell me not to go
around with your daddy, but it is my fate to be with
him. . . .

Love,
Diep

Mrs. Jannice,

. . . I see your picture in his wallet. You are very beautiful lady, very nice. I'm very thin. I want to get some fat, but no do by medicines. Maybe I have to eat much, much better. Oh! The last Friday the V.C. [Viet Cong] attacked the Da Nang airfield. Many people were killed. Very sorry!

Donice, don't worry about your daddy and me. We marry or no. But I hope you wear your Vietnamese dress to your friends and say from friend in Vietnam. O.K.? I hope we be friends and see each other soon.

Love,
Diep

Dear Mrs. Jannice,

I hope this doesn't make you unpleasant and you understand me. My English maybe not so good. I would like to write you and be friendly and write your girl, too. She is sweet. I know her from her picture her daddy show me, and I would like to send her some nice things sometimes.

I love her daddy and he loves me too. I don't know why. It is my fate. I hope you tell me what he likes and how to make him happy. He loved you and was happy. Maybe we can make each other peaceful.

Please say best regard to your other children for me, and tell them that the war in Vietnam will be over some day soon, and perhaps we shall all be together as one. It would be nice if we could see the peace together, your country and mine.

Love,
Diep

I wrote back to her this time. There was something so disarmingly innocent, appealing, and open about her letters. Her friendliness had a warm, childlike quality. With the expectation that we might one day see each other on a regular basis—if she married Ed and came to the States—I responded:

Dear Diep,

Your English is easily understood and you write very well. I, too, wish to be friendly, and I hope you have a good and happy life with Ed and am sure you do not need any advice from me as to how you might make him happy. If you can make each other peaceful, that is wonderful. My daughter Donice is enjoying her school classes and has joined a girl's organization called "The Campfire Girls." This group, like a club, meets weekly at one of the children's homes, and the girls learn many skills from cooking to arts and crafts and athletic activities. My sons are digging an underground fort in our backyard. It is pretty deep, and all three of them can hide there. They were thrilled when I took their dinner and sleeping bags out to them last night. They came inside early this morning, and it was plain that they had not slept very well, but they enjoyed their adventure just the same. . . .

My letter seemed too long when I read it over before putting it in the envelope to mail. Would the children's activities sound ridiculous to her? What similarities were there in our children's activities? Could her children have any kind of normal playtime in Da Nang?

I was relieved when a return letter from her assured me that children in that war-torn country could still play and enjoy their childhood.

Diep's letters to Donice were warm and filled with nostalgia for her own lost childhood.

. . . Thank you for writing to me. What are you doing this summer vacation? I am regretting the school years of the past time. How beautiful they were! When you go on in the life, you will regret the youth and school life that is past. How free and happy I was when my girlhood was spent with the song of children and the carefree days. You will go to the beach this summer? I like the beach. In Da Nang over here we live very close to the beach, but I not go to beach very often anymore. I busy at work now and have much work at library because I am head librarian and I have been at work here four years at library. I love my daily work and I make friendly with the books. I have put down my pen and will write to you again.

Love,
Diep

Dear Little Donice,

I hope you and your brothers have good time this summer. It is very hot in Da Nang and the schools are closing for summer vacation. The examinations are coming to the pupils. The elementary schools are closed in May, and the high schools close in June. Do you go to the beach yet or camping? What do you spend the leisure time? Do you like to needlework? At high school every week we had two hours for learning to needle and cook. How I loved the school life! Do you like some stamps? I sent to you. Maybe my English is too poor? In Vietnam they are learning the English much more than before. My little girls they so cute and sweet. They have the innocent time of childhood now. I pray they always know only the peace and never the pain of war. Many children in my country have no mother or father, and many children die with hunger. I cry for them and hold my children closer. . . .

Diep

"Do you really think he'll bring her back with him?" Dottie asked.

"It's likely," I said. "Judging from her letters, it must be a serious romance at least."

Dottie's face lit up. "The youngest girl . . . could she be his?"

"No chance," I replied. "According to her birthdate, she was conceived before Ed arrived in Vietnam. I only hope he's good to her. Diep is in one bad predicament over there as a single woman with American children."

Dottie made a face and snorted. "I've heard stories about how good the Vietnamese girls are to our servicemen."

"Well, if you were in that situation, what would *you* do?"

"Don't defend it, Janni. It's exploitive!"

"The question is, *who* is doing the exploiting?" I asked, an irritation in my voice that I couldn't hide.

"Did it ever occur to you she's a hooker?"

"No, I'm sure she isn't," I told her. "And if she is, so what?"

"You're impossible!" Dottie vigorously stubbed out her cigarette on a saucer.

Nowadays it seemed that whenever Dottie and I got together, our arguments were always the same.

"Diep seems innocent and sweet from her letters," I told Dottie.

"Hmmmm. You're pretty naive, Janni. She has two half-American kids already. At best, I bet she's a hostess in a club, and Ed is just one more meal ticket for her."

"Even so, I sense that she's a decent and fine person."

"That's the idealist and romantic speaking," Dottie said kiddingly. "She's a survivor. Women in war will do anything they have to in order to guarantee that they and their kids eat.''

"Well, can you fault them for that?'' I asked my usual question.

"Of course not, but let's be realistic. She's no angel. I'll wager you that her letters to you and Donice are not just simple letters from a would-be pen pal. She's feathering her nest any way that she can.''

"That's ridiculous!'' My irritation showed.

"Maybe, but true, I'll bet. That's an insane situation over there. Without help from some poor romantic American, Diep is a goner.'' Dottie shook her head. "Don't you see? As an employee for our government in that library and the mother of two half-American kids, she's not on any Viet Cong Most Popular Girl of the Year List.''

The terrible implication of her words finally sank in.

"We'll win that war; why on the news just last night—''

"Janni, that's a pipe dream. We're being creamed over there. I predict that our troops will pull out within the year. You'll see.''

"Then Ed'll bring her and her little girls over here. I just know he will.'' But how could I know any such thing?

Not long after, in November of 1967, a letter arrived from Diep saying that Ed was on his way to the United States to see us on an "R & R,'' that he would be here in a few weeks. She wanted me to tell him that she missed him and loved him, and she would be waiting anxiously for his return.

When Ed arrived at our home, Larry met him at the door. They exchanged stiff but polite greetings. Ed was tanned and relaxed; he looked like a man who had just returned from a vacation resort, and that is exactly how he described Vietnam—as a resort. He talked about the beach at Da Nang and how graceful and feminine the women there were.

Then he pulled out photographs of Diep's little girls, and, holding Donice on his lap, showed them to her.

"How would you like to have two little stepsisters?" he asked her. She shrugged the way children do when they don't know how to react.

"Is that an announcement?" I asked him, smiling. Diep must be the bright light in his life, I decided.

"Could be." He returned the smile. "In the future, maybe," he added mysteriously.

"That's great." I was sincerely enthusiastic.

It wasn't until he started to leave and the children had gone outside to play that Ed told me that "things aren't really going too well over there."

I must have looked surprised. "I thought we were winning the war?"

He shook his head, saying that he could foresee a day when we would be pulling out, although at the moment there were over 500,000 Americans in Vietnam.

"When and if the day arrives that the Americans leave," he told me, "there will be a real *bloodbath* over there." His eyes were dead and expressionless.

"Diep and her children will be coming here, though?"

"I honestly don't know at this point," he replied.

"But if not . . . I mean, what about them?"

"That's war," he said.

Believing that Ed and Diep were still deeply involved, I was stunned. The tone of her letters had indicated that something was seriously wrong, but I had no clue as to what it could be.

By now Diep and I were exchanging photos and gifts on a regular basis. It seemed to me that we were beginning to share a closeness that contrasted sharply with Ed's casual dismissal.

December 4, 1967

Dear Diep,

How adorable your children are in the photo I have by my typewriter. Yes, your older child is close to my Marna in age. I also have your photo wearing the lovely and graceful *ao dai*. I wish that style was popular in the U.S.A. It is so feminine and comfortable-looking.

We are the same height, but you're right about being smaller. Less than ninety pounds, you say? Well, we must wear the same-size shoe, because the red shoes you sent me from Saigon fit quite well. Thank you so much.

Jann

January 13, 1968

Dear Mrs. Jannice,

Thank you for the letter and the photographs. Your boys are nice and handsome. Two have the blond hair and one the dark. I saw a young boy from your home and I ask him if he know you. He said he did, then I told him when you go home, you let me send something with you for Mrs. Jannice please. He said "one more year" and look so sad. I have the pity on him. He is so young, maybe 18 or 19. His friends they smoke the drugg [sic] or "opium," I don't know how to call it. It very dangerous and can make you crazy. I saw young American boys smoke it and look terrible. The eyes turn red, skin turn very dark, look like no blood and the death face, and they do not know when to stop the smoking and needle and sometimes they just die. It is sad to die fighting, but it is even sadder to die from the drugg. Well, this war is very worst, not same as the Second

World War. I am afraid we have a Third World War now, and it be in our country first. Then all of Vietnam will be swallowed by the ocean and will be lost forever.

Love,
Diep

Dear Diep,

Here are some photographs taken two weeks ago of the children and their dog, "Siggie." I am sending a box of children's clothes, some of them new and others in excellent condition but outgrown by my children. If your little girls like them I will be happy. If not, perhaps there are children whom you know that could use them. Thank you for the handbag. It is beautiful! Your last letter mentioned the drugs that soldiers take over there, and our news here tells us that there is considerable drug use among our boys. I share your sadness over this, and hope the young man you mentioned from my neighborhood will escape this problem. I suppose that frightened and lonely soldiers try to escape the problem of their fear and loneliness with the drug, which only creates a worse and more lasting problem itself.

Jann

Our letters passed back and forth with friendly regularity now. I looked forward to them, enthusiastic when a colorfully decorated enveloped with the bright Vietnamese stamps appeared in my mailbox. As the nightly TV news showed even worse and more incomprehensible horrors in Vietnam, I found an outlet in sending small packages of needed items to Diep and her children. The ever-growing anxiety over the war permeated every periodical and news report, and now more and more American families felt the tragedy of this war. By sending aspirin or children's

clothes to Diep, I felt I was doing something to ease my
personal grief about it. My continuous contact with a
woman who was right in the middle of the horror gave me
an awful vicarious sense of what it would be like, and my
strong maternal feelings made me identify with her, the
mother of two little girls whose lives might also be in
danger. I just couldn't imagine the trauma of having children in such a perilous situation and fending for them all
alone.

Marna's serious illness made me even more sensitive to
Diep's anxieties about her children. Every day I awoke
with an unvoiced question about my youngest child's future. It was not a question about what *kind* of future she
would have, but whether or not she would have a future at
all. A mother who heard rockets exploding nearby
throughout her days and evenings, who saw death regularly, who witnessed pain and suffering and saw the misery
of homeless children, would ask the same questions about
her beloved children that I asked myself about Marna.
Each morning when I awoke to hear that familiar choking
cough, it was—for me—like a rocket exploding somewhere too close to the baby I loved so much.

In April of 1967 I returned from yet another visit to the
hospital, this time fighting an infection that had never been
controlled following surgery, to find Diep's friendly letter
awaiting me.

Dear Mrs. Jannice,

How sorry am I that you be sick. I worry. I wish that
I could be there to help take care of you. I would love
that. I would clean your house and care for the children
and do all things to help you get well.

Da Nang is holding the wet season now. It is hot, but

the rains still come. Everything is clean and new after the rains.

"Would you be mean to her if he brought her here?" Donice wanted to know.

"Why on earth would I be mean to her?"

"Would you be jealous, Mama?"

"Of course not. I'm not his wife any longer. I'm married to Larry. I don't feel any anger or resentment, and I don't feel possessive, either."

"What is 'possessive'?" my daughter asked as we cleared the table and stacked the dinner dishes.

"Ownership. Feeling as if your father somehow belongs to me. Married people often feel that way, which isn't wrong, I suppose. But all of that is long over."

She was silent. In her eight-year-old mind she was trying to sort out many grown-up things. Then she said, "I think Daddy is possessive of *you*. I think he feels he owns you and us."

"You may be right, but why do you say that?"

"Because of his letters. They don't sound like he knows we love Larry." She paused. "I want to call Larry 'Daddy.' Is that all right?"

Despite our rough beginnings, Larry had adjusted to instant fatherhood quickly. He was the father of two girls from his previous marriage, and when they visited us, we squired around a brood of seven. He still could not get used to entering a restaurant with all those kids in tow. ("People will think I don't know what causes pregnancy," he would say.) Although he loved the children, their actual number continued to embarrass him in public.

In our home peanut butter was a staple, and lunchtime was not lunchtime unless there were peanut-butter sand-

wiches. The first time Larry saw my mass-produced sandwiches, he lost his appetite. There was no finesse to my
style, he told me. Where he carefully spread peanut butter
from one corner of the bread slice to the others, avoiding
lumps, I slapped it on as quickly as possible, sometimes
leaving globs in the center in my haste. His sandwiches
were placed neatly on the plate, uniform in thickness, cut
diagonally. Those that I made for "The Troops" were
piled up on a tray in stacks and offered to the squabbling
soldiers, who devoured them almost as fast as I could make
them.

Soups and stews—the kind you make from what's in the
refrigerator—were often on the menu. My idea of afford-
able luxury was "Jerry's Beefburger Special: 5 for $1"
Larry was the practical one, with good nutrition his cri-
terion for good meals. The fact that his soups and stews
were nutritious made them less palatable to the kids,
however. They were collectively suspicious about the in-
gredients.

"If it doesn't move, eat it!" was the dictum they imag-
ined to be their stepfather's creed. They were envious of
two neighborhood boys who finished off *their* lunches with
Hostess Twinkies and tortilla chips.

For several years after our marriage, well-meaning
friends of Larry remained doubtful about his judgment.
They had solicitously offered to seek help for him when
he first announced that he was marrying a woman with
five children. When Larry gave up the Porsche, one friend
suggested I'd placed a hex on him; when we drove up in
the coughing Rambler wagon, that same man was convinced. A Volkswagen Bug replaced the Rambler eventually, and Larry removed the back seat so that all the
children could fit in the back. They sat on boarded "tiers,"

usually indignant, as they didn't want to be different from their friends, who sat on real car seats.

Larry continued to be self-conscious about The Troops when we were out in public. One evening I had to drop off a book at the home of a casual acquaintance. Her husband came out to the car to greet us. He shook hands with Larry, then peered with astonishment into our car and invited us all inside.

"A drink, perhaps?" he asked, looking hesitantly at his wife, then at our children, and back at us. "You *must* drink, with all those kids!"

At home, the noise level was often like a school playground at noon. When I first met Larry, he lived the life of a serene bachelor in a tree-shaded neighborhood whose homes were set far back from the street. His small rented house seemed nearly buried in shrubbery, and it was surrounded by gigantic redwoods. In those days it was his habit to come home from work and retreat into that secluded house, undisturbed. For a long time, he did not even have a phone.

When he married me, those days of serenity were gone forever. The only truly quiet time was when the children slept.

With two years between each of my kids—like skipped rungs on a wobbly ladder—sibling competition was a constant. Someone always had someone else's something. Someone always had more of something than the next child. (I once read in *Parent's* Magazine that the best way to teach a child how to count was to give his sibling one more grape than you gave him.) Such dilemmas were always handled by noisy contests, with Larry or me as referee.

Chapter Four

Storm Clouds East and West

"How would you like to do your intern teaching at Diablo Valley College?" As Norris Pope, dean of instruction, asked the question, my heart began to beat faster. Surely he could hear it. He had the kindest face, the gentlest eyes I had ever seen. I tried to seem calm, poised, but with a dream beginning to come true, it was impossible. I gushed out my happiness, and we talked about the paperwork and necessary arrangements.

I would teach one section of freshman composition. I was already enrolled in graduate courses at San Francisco State College and had a thesis to write the following summer. My work was certainly cut out for me.

Larry was pleased with my news. Diablo Valley College was only three miles from home, and since I had graduated from there, I was already familiar with the campus.

"Of course my real dream is to be permanent there one day," I told Larry. "Now that dream seems very close."

"Well, Honey, 1968 may be your lucky year! You've earned it, I might say. Oh, by the way, Marni woke up this morning with a slight fever. Think it could mean something new?"

"I'd better give her another therapy before I go to school tonight. She's been producing more mucus during therapy, and it seems to have changed color."

"Tell you what." Larry mixed the enzymes in her food as Marna sat quietly in her chair, watching him. "If you give her therapy now, I'll give her a double one before putting her to bed tonight." Larry seemed to "pound" harder on her little body, but she usually put up with it good-naturedly because she loved him so much. When he did the therapy, the suctioning that she hated often wasn't needed either.

"No want . . . no want tarpy . . ." Marni started to cry, rubbing her eyes. "NO want tarpy, jus' EAT." She reached aggressively for the food that was already blackening from the enzymes.

I fought an impulse to give in. I had been having migraine headaches, which the doctors told me were stress related. They were becoming worse and worse, often incapacitating me for days at a time. The strength that lifting Marna and administering her therapy required left me exhausted. Sometimes I ached all over at the end of a day, especially when three therapy sessions were required. It would have been easy to give in to her, but I knew we couldn't.

In 1968, university students across the nation were becoming militant, with sit-ins and vandalism frequent occurrences at the major universities. San Francisco State followed suit. Whenever I went to school in those days, action groups were gathered on campus. Sometimes

speakers ranted and shouted their messages at eager crowds
of students, whipping them into revolt and even violence.
President Bob Smith stepped down and his vacancy was
filled by a tamo-o'shanter-crowned Japanese-Canadian
named S. I. Hayakawa.

Dr. Hayakawa was my semantics professor. One afternoon I was in his office when a truck of student protesters
pulled up outside. Hearing someone shouting obscenities
at him, Hayakawa abruptly left the office, tam-o'-shanter
on his head, and climbed aboard the truck. The sight of
him grabbing the bullhorn away from a protester, yanking
wires and equipment out, and tossing them off the truck,
will forever be in my memory. It was also to become a
now-famous photograph in the newspapers the next day.

After a graduate seminar one cold and windy evening
just before sunset, I was hurrying home on a five-lane
freeway from San Francisco. I was driving about 70 miles
an hour—the speed limit was higher then—when a car just
ahead of me in the next lane suddenly pulled in front of
me.

The driver was going much slower. I swerved to avoid
hitting him, and my car struck the gravel on the shoulder
of the highway, then fishtailed and turned over, spinning
upside down across five lanes of traffic. By the time my
poor old Volkswagen came to rest at the side of the road
against an embankment it looked as if a blowtorch had
gone over it. Weeping, I slid out of the passenger-side
window, not knowing the extent of my injuries.

With no seat belt on, I had clung desperately to the
steering wheel when the Volks spun out of control. The
entire interior of the car was an orange-red from the sparks
caused by the car's grinding on asphalt. For a few long
seconds I was sure I was going to die. It was an oddly

calm feeling, a detached sadness that I would be leaving Larry to care for five children so soon after our marriage.

The miracle that I lived through the accident was due to the fact that no other auto had hit me as I spun across the freeway. Luckily for me, it was an hour after the peak commuter traffic. I was disheveled but composed when the ambulance arrived to take me to Mission Emergency Hospital. The car was so badly damaged that it should have been junked—if we could have afforded another car. The hospital called Larry, and he arrived an hour after I had been admitted for observation.

"How are you feeling?" Larry was by my side at the hospital.

"Numb . . . scared . . ." I began. Tears filled my eyes, and I averted my head so he would not see me cry.

"Any results from the X-rays yet?" Larry asked soberly.

I told him no. "The doctor says that sometimes it takes time before one realizes what damage has taken place. He said that the insurance company representing the man who caused my accident will probably get hold of me immediately, hoping I'll want to settle right away. His advice was to wait a while."

"Good advice," Larry said stonily. "It's a surprise to me that the guy who caused you to go out of control actually pulled over. He easily could have kept going."

"And he was so young, and his wife and baby were in his car," I said. "I wish it were possible to reward people who pull over like that, rather than penalize them. I'm afraid that his insurance company won't be too pleased with him, the way he instantly admitted liability to the highway patrol."

"Well, I'll call the college first thing in the morning and cancel——"

"No!" I told Larry. "I'm sure this is just minor. I was so lucky. I'll make my class tomorrow."

But by morning my neck throbbed with such intense pain that I could barely move. Larry made the call after all.

In the days to follow, the pain was so severe that I had to miss many classes. Now the migraines took over my life with a fury. If I lifted Marna or bent over or even hung clothes out to dry, the pain in my neck seemed to trigger a headache that began instantly and sent me helpless to my bed, with ice packs. The relentless throbbing pain left me vomiting, often nearly senseless. I evaluated my days by the intensity of the headaches and whether or not I had been able to accomplish even the smallest tasks.

"All I can offer you are muscle relaxants and painkillers," my doctor said. "Of course, you pay a price when you get rid of pain. Your thinking may be fuzzy at first, until you become accustomed to the drugs."

"So I'm licked no matter what I do?" It was more a statement than a question: I knew the answer. With the misery of a headache I could only stay quiet in bed and suffer. Without it, I might at least be able to function.

Sometimes the agony was so horrible that nothing could touch it. I vomited up pills, and after hours of dry-heaving, I was too dehydrated and ill to tolerate anything more than a shot of Demerol in the emergency room at the hospital. My compassionate doctor, realizing that these emergency room "waits" contributed to the intensity of the headaches and represented expenses we could not afford in the first place, began prescribing Demerol injections, which Larry could administer to me at home.

Larry had never had any interest in medicine or doctoring. Since he seemed to suffer more than I when he jabbed me with those long needles, I soon took over the administering of the drug. When soon—very soon—it became necessary to give myself shots more frequently, I denied that a new trouble was just beginning for me, even though my intelligence whispered the awful truth. I even mentioned it to Diep.

Dear Diep,
   I've had an auto accident. That's why I haven't written. It's to a point where I have to give myself shots. . . . I'm never free of pain, except when I take the shots. . . .

The Demerol made it possible for me to stay up long hours studying, free of pain. The Demerol made it possible for me to give Marna therapy without aching the entire time. It seemed miraculous that I could feel so wonderful only seconds after having felt such agony before the shot.

"The drugs just cover up the problem," Larry said after dinner one evening. "You know that."

"So far I've been to four specialists since the accident, and when they learn something about my family life, particularly when they know I have five children and am enrolled in college . . ."

"And one of your kids has cystic fibrosis . . ." Larry added.

"Yes, then they say, *'Of course* you have headaches, Mrs. Jansen. Have you ever thought of taking life easier?' "

"Just the same," Larry said sadly, "drugs don't eliminate the cause of migraines. Now, perhaps stress has something to do with them, but the headaches have become much worse since the accident. A friend was telling me about a doctor he knows . . ."

The following morning, holding an ice pack to my forehead, I managed to dial the number of the recommended doctor for an appointment. As I did, I wondered how long I would be able to tolerate this headache, now worsening by the minute, without another shot.

"You're the eighth doctor I've seen about the headaches," I told the stern-faced man seated across the room.

"I'm afraid that I can't tell you anything the others haven't already covered, judging from your history," he said.

"The last doctor said I'd be on drug therapy for the rest of my life," I told him, fighting back the tears.

He shrugged his shoulders. After a long silence he said, "That's likely, but I hate to see a woman as young as you are having to take so many painkillers and muscle relaxants. You've been to physical therapy?"

I nodded, still fighting the tears that threatened to embarrass me. It seemed I had been everywhere. To so many specialists!

"You've spent . . . how many months in a cervical collar? Six? Eight? Hmmm. Well, your X-rays were taken immediately following the accident. Sometimes bruised or swollen tissues hide things. Tell you what: I'll have some X-rays taken of your neck, and we'll see what they tell us now that so many months have passed since you got hurt."

Larry waited for me in the car while the X-rays were taken. He was beginning to wear a permanent expression of resignation, which frightened me. The severity of the headaches was taking me out of the real world and into a dizzying one of blackouts, depression, and drugs that consumed my days, smothered me with guilt, and kept me pacing for hours at night when I was not spending what seemed like hours retching. The pain and the narcotic still nauseated me. The dosage of the drug had increased considerably, even more so under my own administration. The physician who gave me the prescription was unaware of my progressing dilemma: I was wracked by severe pain that required strong medication, which I came to need more and more as my addiction grew. A compassionate man, he probably just did not know what to do for me. The fact that I "needed" the narcotic more and more often did alarm him, however.

I "needed" Demerol when Marna's physical therapy had me doubled over in agony as I did each position and had to lift her. I "needed" it each time I had to admit her to the hospital, which was happening more and more often. I "needed" it when I had to leave her behind. I "needed" it each time I answered the door to a court officer serving another summons to pull me into court about selling the house, Ed's new demand on me now that I was remarried. Our divorce settlement had stated that if I ever remarried, I would have to sell the family home. Larry and I wanted to find another place of our own, but our depleted finances and my worsening health, as well as Marna's, made us helpless to make changes. Ed was not in financial trouble, but Larry and I were. Soon I no longer knew which pain I was trying to escape, the physical or the emotional.

My world seemed filled with overwhelming problems, and that fuzzy, sleepy daze through which I stumbled insulated me from pain of all kinds. It also insulated me from the wonderful aspects of life that offer levity and balance.

No matter how zapped I was, Larry's mood or facial expression always came through. He could spot my Demerol daze from any distance, and it made him turn cold with fear, anger, and frustration. His rejection drove me to seek unconsciousness even more.

One evening after I had taken at least four shots and was wandering about the house trying to tidy up little bits of clutter I had just caused, I had one of my waking dreams. It was mostly about Russ, a thirty-year-old man who lived next door and was dying of leukemia. In the dream I kept talking to him, weeping to myself. I kept "seeing" him in our house, although he was really in the hospital at the time. In my waking dream, I kept seeing Russ and saying Marna's name.

I stood in front of the bathroom mirror and said to the unfamiliar image that now stared back at me:

"MARNI IS GOING TO DIE. SHE AND RUSS . . ."

Suddenly Larry walked into my dream. "I just can't handle this anymore," he said softly, his eyes cold as he looked at my unrecognizable mirror image.

Later, a letter from Diep brought a hopeful message.

Dear Mrs. Jannice,

Thank you for the yarn and clothes you sent me over here. My little girls, so sweet and cute, will now have clothes to keep them warm. How is your little Marni? Your last letter say she not doing well. Be O.K. She will be fine and your headaches will go.

Love,
Diep

Her optimism warmed me. Shortly after I had received her letter, my doctor called.

"The good news is that we've found what is probably the cause of all your pain," he told me. "The bad news is that surgery is definitely indicated—it may or may not alleviate your suffering."

My heart pounded. Thank God he didn't say it was my imagination! "You have four ruptured discs," he said.

"No doubt about it. Small wonder you've been in such pain."

"We don't have the money for any operation," I told Larry after dinner that night. "So I'll just have to hang in there until we do."

"It's not as though we have any choice," Larry replied. "On the other hand, you can't go on like this. I can't, for that matter. Knowing that you had a ten-mile drive ahead of you, when you left in the morning to substitute-teach, I was almost frantic, wondering if you'd had a shot before you got into that car."

"You know that I don't take medication when I go to work," I said, irritated.

"I don't know anything of the kind. When you're in as much pain as you claim to be, how do I know what you'll do to relieve it?"

"Trust me not to take anything before going to work," I said quietly, feeling the frightened tension build in the back of my neck as muscles tightened and blood vessels began to swell. The headache was threatening to return after nearly two days of relief.

I dashed into the bathroom and gave myself a shot. Now at least I could give Marna her evening therapy without doubling over in agony, sparing Larry from having to do it. After I had a shot or two or three, I could—with glorious relief—write marvelous letters that I would discover were illegible the following morning. I could concoct exotic dinners for my family from a dozen eggs mixed with catsup and blended with a large can of dog food. (This bizarre behavior became a family joke later on, but when I was first told about what I had done—having had amnesia about the event—I was horrified.) I could move about with the freedom from pain most people take for granted, fall asleep soundly . . . until the pain that woke me was so excruciating that I headed for another shot of Demerol, then on to the bathroom to throw up.

Sometimes I busied myself around the house, doing nothing in particular but driven by a need to do something, to keep myself from letting my life waste away. Larry would have to force me to go to bed, but when I was in this condition he would not sleep with me. Often I became determined to clean my house, though I couldn't see the vacuum cleaner through the confused blur. I was determined that now that the pain had subsided, I could accomplish all the things that had previously been beyond my pain-filled consciousness.

No matter how sick I was, however, I always sobered when my children needed me for something, from baking cookies for a school class—*without* dog food as an ingredient—to giving one of them a piano lesson. No matter how drugged I was, I was clearly focused on Marna's needs, and the anger and fear in Larry's eyes always penetrated my haze, sending a shock of agonizing guilt and despair through me.

One evening as I drifted off into a troubled Demerol-induced sleep, my friend Dottie phoned.

"You all right?" she asked with concern, detecting something strange about my voice. I assured her that I was fine.

"I just thought you should know, in case you're not watching the news. Da Nang is apparently really getting it. Bombing. Fires . . . it's awful!"

As if on cue, a letter came from Diep the following day:

Dear Jannice,

For a long time I didn't write, but I always think of you and your kindness . . . We are in the war, always war, war. The next generation of Vietnamese is in the

dark, will never progress. But we are O.K. now, and in
convenience situation. We just worry about the war
around us and our future. Viet Cong always attack at
night in Da Nang, which is still off limits. . . . Many
got wounded last night . . . many nice houses got fired
to ground by V.C., and I ask God to please save us. . . .

Almost every day now, we were witness to the chaos
on television. We heard the sounds of people yelling, saw
the heavily armed soldiers diving into tall grasses, the men
being hastily carried out on stretchers dead and dying,
blood everywhere . . . Saw the toddlers huddled under a
lean-to, hungry, stoic, with the eyes of small, wounded
wild animals; saw the anguished face of a mother nursing
her baby against a gutted building, her leg wrapped in
bandages; heard the popping sounds of artillery in the distance, as people came running across the street into a
building. All were images of war, images that made me
hold my own children closer and wonder why it had to be.

"Dottie called," Larry announced one afternoon. "Her
nephew, Scotty MacLeod, just got back from Saigon. He's
been hurt, though not too seriously. Do you want to see
him? You might learn more about Vietnam."

Although my neck felt as though someone had struck
me with a hammer, and the constant pounding in my tem-
ples, the mounting nausea, were the threatening headache's conspirators, I was determined to see Scotty.
Another letter from Diep had arrived that afternoon. The
tone of her letters had changed from happy-in-love optimism to bitterness over her belief that Ed had betrayed
and abandoned her. I found myself thinking about this
woman a great deal. There was something akin to guilt
connected to my worry about her. Despite the problems I
faced, never had I known the life-threatening experiences

she was facing daily. If I was ever to offer up my life for anything, it would have been for the lives and safety of my children, and here she was, a loving mother, fearing for the lives of her children every day.

In spite of the migraine, I wanted to know more. "Sure, I'd like to meet Scotty."

"Are you feeling up to company?" Larry looked concerned, that mix of frustration and fear in his eyes that I recognized so keenly meant he knew a migraine was coming on.

"Yes, I'm all right," I lied.

Scotty was in his early twenties, with the face of a young boy and the manner of someone who had acquired considerable street sense and sophistication. He took Dottie's maternal hovering in stride. When he mentioned that just as soon as he recuperated from his leg injuries he planned to return to Vietnam, she exploded, but he brushed off her protests affectionately.

"I love those people," he said with feeling. "They really need our help, and when I came home to see all the demonstrations and stuff, you can't know how I felt." He crushed a beer can in his hands absentmindedly. "Besides, I met a girl over there. . . ." He hesitated, looking at Dottie and catching the silent message of reproach in her eyes.

"Dot says that your ex-old man's been over there," he said amiably.

He looked quickly at Larry to see if he had hit a sensitive spot. To put him at ease, Larry said, "Ed's been with the USO. Jann's been corresponding with the woman he's involved with. We're worried about her."

"Where's she living?" Scotty asked.

"Da Nang," I told him.

Scotty winced. "It's getting pretty hot there now," he

said solemnly. "Refugees are beginning to flood into Da Nang from the Central Highlands, too. There's hunger. Fear. It's bad," he said with a faraway look in his eyes, as if he were trying to see Vietnam from our kitchen table.

"I'll bet Ed has already dumped that Vietnamese girl," Dottie said with disgust.

Scotty came to his defense quickly. "Hey, Dot, don't be so quick to put him on trial."

Dottie shrugged and inhaled deeply on her cigarette.

"Seriously"—Scotty turned toward her—"you just don't know what it's like over there, especially for the women and kids. You said yesterday that she's got American kids? Well, the only way she'll ever get out of that hole alive is if she can find some American to help her. Maybe Jann's ex-husband took up with her just so he could help her."

"That's a likely story." Dottie snorted. Larry and I said nothing.

"Well, it's possible that he married her to help her," I said softly. Three heads came up quickly.

"Married her?" Dottie and Larry asked in unison. I nodded.

"In her letter over there"—I gestured toward the familiar-looking envelope with "USO Army Library" printed in the upper-left corner—"Diep says that they were officially married. She expressed concern that he might have tired of her already; he is gone a great deal and she sees very little of him. She doesn't say that he has abandoned her, however, although I'm sure that she's afraid of that."

There was a long silence.

"Well, I've considered marrying my little gal when I go back, and if things don't work out, at least I will have brought her to the safety of the good old US of A," Scotty said. "You may never know, but it could be that your ex-old man is trying to work things out in his mind about how she'll fit in and all. Give him the benefit of the doubt," he added.

Days blended together, one indistinguishable from the next. Marna's cheeks were pink from sun and activity, and I was very grateful. She played more vigorously with her brothers and sister than I had ever seen her do before. She was giggling and happy. At times when she was out of breath, she dissolved into a fit of coughing, but she didn't seem as bothered by the coughing as before. Now when I watched her I frequently felt a surge of happiness and hope.

The next letter from Diep upset me. It seemed to confirm Dottie's view of Ed.

. . . I don't know why I loved him. He somehow made me love him. He tried hard to follow me, and if he leaves me here, I thought he is so brutal with me! He said he is still very hurt to lose you, and don't let him lose me, too. He tried to make marry certificate at City Hall, so on the paper I am his wife. If he leaves me, I can't marry because of the law. Do you think he is disloyal? I hope he has conscience and concern and is human. He will be punished if he does bad with me. . . . If somehow I am not in his life, I still would like to write you in friendly. I always respect you. I hope you understand me. My friends help me to send you two calendars, one for you and one for your little daughter.
　　　　　　　　　　　　　　　　Yours respectfully,
　　　　　　　　　　　　　　　　Diep

"What do you think?" I asked Larry.
"I think that after he married her, he changed his mind

and decided it was a mistake, or else he figured that now it was easier for her to get out of Vietnam, so he could take off.''

''You also believe that he's taken off?'' I asked.

Larry nodded. ''It's a good hunch,'' he said solemnly. ''Obviously she thinks so.''

The following month another letter came.

> . . . I'll see the consular, but it isn't easy for me to get divorce without him. You try to find him for me? I think he is hiding. The truth is I did not ask the consular before because I was ashamed and afraid that they would say I was bad. . . . My heart is very cold to him now. Before I tried to love him. It was my fate. I wanted to see U.S. and find a new life for my poor naive children. Perhaps if he be found, he hurt my children's feelings later. I must know that one day I will be divorced. The papers of marriage he made for me, but I changed my mind. I only want to go to U.S. I am still young, but I don't want more men because I never want to hurt my poor children. I never want to answer the questions my smart children will ask me. . . . My first daughter, she same age as your Marna, and she is cute and sweet like your daughter's picture.

''Don't be so tough on him,'' Randy admonished Dottie when she let out some four-letter words after reading Diep's latest letter. ''Remember, he might have married her simply with the intention of making it easier for her to get out of that place, but he never had any plans for living with her for good. A lot of guys have done that.''

''Then why doesn't he at least keep in touch with the poor woman?'' Dottie whirled around as if to charge her husband.

"Take it easy. Take it easy." He put up his hands as if to defend himself. "Look, I'm not sticking up for him. I'm only trying to say that . . ."

"Hey, guys," I said calmly, "we can't actually know what the situation is. What puzzles me is that some of Diep's letters seem so . . . matter of fact. She mentions the war and alludes to her situation in one letter, then really pours it on in the next. I can't get a good fix on exactly what her situation really is."

"Don't be so naive," Dottie said. "You know she's in one helluva predicament, and you're her only hope now."

"Thanks a lot. You were the one who thought I should just bow out of this and stop writing to her long ago, weren't you?" Now *I* was feeling testy.

Dottie shook her head with frustration. "Yeah, but now it's different." She said it so softly that I could barely hear her. "Now she's a real person, someone you are . . . almost committed to."

I knew she was right. The next letter from Vietnam confirmed it even more.

My Dearest Mrs. Jannice,

How kind you are to us here. Thank you for the vitamins and aspirin. You are like a true sister to me, perhaps better than a sister. I shall find no better.

Da Nang is still off limits. Although no V.C. in town, the V.C. tried to attack, but they never win and just killed people around the country. V.C. had paid high, 27,000 V.C. died in South Vietnam in two weeks attacking all cities. Some cities are occupied by V.C. already. In Vietnam there are four places that we can attend the college: Hue, Saigon, Da Lat and Nga Trang. Do you like biologie [sic]? That is my subject. I love the science. . . . Over here we didn't have many subjects and many colleges will open everywhere in my country when war is over as in the U.S.A. I hope so. *Now my country is burning by the war. Every day I see the death of my country, the pain and the death. The country, it is occupied by Viet Cong and people are hungry.* The V.C. are poor. They don't like the rich.

I get very busy with two little girls. I thought of how you get so busy with five children. I hope they be good and don't cause you trouble. I worry about my girls so much. . . .

Diep

I remember how I fixed a big turkey that last happy Thanksgiving of 1968, and the children's godparents joined us for dinner. Marna stretched out on the couch—listless, weary, and definitely showing signs of coming down with an infection. I had come to dread the changes in the weather, the bitterly cold, frosty mornings following early autumn, and the wind. Most of all, I dreaded the wind. It seemed to be the harbinger of her infections, infections that would only make normal children ill but could mean hospitalization and serious complications for Marna.

I'll never forget that Thanksgiving. At the end of the day, after children were tucked into bed and guests had gone home, I called a baby-sitter, and Larry and I took Marna to the hospital. She buried her face in my coat as I held her close all the way on that long, twenty-three-mile drive. Hot tears streamed down my face and down my throat as I wept silently in fear.

Two weeks later she came home, still depressed, breathing hard and coughing harder. We stepped up her therapy sessions, and the strain and worry kept me in constant physical pain as well. By now I had built up a tolerance to the drugs, and only Larry had any idea how much I was taking in order to function without the debilitating pain of migraine headaches.

I was tutoring at home as well as substitute teaching for three school districts, so I was receiving early morning request calls nearly every day. Substitute teaching worked well for me; if Marna were coming down with an infection or when her brothers or sister were ill, I could turn down these morning requests without concern. However, the considerable stress connected with that kind of teaching certainly aggravated my headaches, which were now constant. I was also teaching piano lessons in the afternoons and some evenings. Larry tried to make his insurance job pay off, but he discovered that for him selling was hardly enjoyable anymore. Although he sincerely believed in what he was doing, he disliked the prospecting and cold calls, and after a while he dreaded nearly every aspect of his work. If it had been more profitable for him, he would probably have been able to tough it out, but I was becoming more and more aware that he needed a change.

Diep's letters continued to come from Vietnam, sealed in recycled envelopes (they were turned inside out). I encouraged her to leave Vietnam. We didn't have much money, I told her, but if she could get me information about what it would take to get her and the children out, I could take it from there. How naive I was in those days.

In June of 1969, American planes made their first raids against North Vietnam since the bombing halt of November 1968, in retaliation for shooting down a reconnaissance aircraft. The most positive news for Americans, and the worst possible news for the South Vietnamese, was President Nixon's announcement that he planned to withdraw 25,000 American combat troops.

* * *

Marna LeAnn was hospitalized for a "routine" hospitalization on June 3, 1969. The plan was to give her more aggressive physical therapies, which could be managed in a hospital. I think her doctor had something else in mind, too; he felt sorry for me and wanted "to give Mama a rest."

This was a different experience for Marna, however. She did not respond as quickly to the medications and hospital treatment as she had formerly, and each day I visited her she seemed more listless and weary than the day before.

"We're suggesting that she have a pulmonary washout," her doctor said one evening when I met him during his rounds. "This often acts as a super physical therapy, and kiddies go home much sooner."

"I've heard that the washouts make the lungs lose their elasticity," I said, "and I've heard that there is a great danger with the procedure."

He shook his head. "To the contrary. In a case like Marna's, it may be the only way to bring her relief. Of course, whenever you have someone suffering from lung disease, the use of an anesthetic is always somewhat risky, but we have the best people here to administer it."

"What are my options?" I asked him.

"Well, she's not doing well, and things could certainly take a turn for the worse. I strongly advise you to give us permission for the washout. Really."

It was agreed that I would come back in the morning and sign the paper giving them permission and that Marna would have the procedure early. When I left the hospital that night, one of the nurses, who loved Marna very much, followed me out to my car. "Don't worry about the strike," she said reassuringly.

"What strike?"

"There's going to be a nurses' strike beginning tomorrow. But don't worry about it. We'll have nurses called in from the registry who're capable and knowledgeable, and the washout is a relatively simple thing, which shouldn't take too long. You'll have your baby home before you know it."

Marna was aware that something different was about to happen to her. She seemed unusually fretful when the nurse came in with the permission paper for me to sign. When a doctor and another nurse returned with a gurney and lifted her onto it, she let out a wail. I clung to her crib for support, fighting the tears with all my might as she was taken off, crying, *"Mama! Mama, don't leave me!"*

I waited for a long time—how long I don't know before she was brought back into her room with an I.V. pole and tubes in her arm and nose. "She won't be able to talk with the tubes down her trachea," one of the nurses said kindly. "In a couple of days it'll be removed, but for now it's necessary."

I noticed that her hands were tied to the sides of the bed, and as Marna struggled to free herself, I requested that she be untied.

"I'm sorry, Mrs. Jansen. We can't have her pulling the tubing out."

"But . . . she's accustomed to having I.V. tubes in her arms," I protested. "She's never pulled one out so far."

The nurse had a warning look in her eyes that told me to be careful if I did not want to be told to leave. Marna's eyes pleaded with me, and I tried to explain to her why she had to be tied up. As she continued to look at me imploringly, I turned my face away so she could not see my tears. Suddenly I realized that she wasn't struggling any longer, and I looked down to see her sad eyes gazing with understanding into mine. She knew I was crying in sympathy with her, and that was enough to quiet her.

The following five days remain a nightmare that still recurs in my dreams at unexpected times. No matter how many years pass, the agony of those five days will remain in my mental library, to be immediate reference whenever I meet another grieving parent who needs my comfort or understanding.

I had believed Marna suddenly looked better, more relaxed. She was not struggling against the machinery as before. Then an angry, sad, and frustrated woman doctor arrived, summoned by one of the nurses. She held a flashlight to Marna's pupils. I didn't understand.

"We want to shut the respirator off, Mrs. Jansen. She's not tripping it by herself any longer." I still didn't understand until the doctor said half-angrily: "Let's stop this. Just STOP this!" During that terrible silence following the unplugging of the machine, I realized Marna was not breathing. The shock as I gazed at the stunned nurses and doctor sent me reeling back against the wall. *Disbelief.*

"I want to hold her one last time," I sobbed. This was not real. Everything had a nightmare quality, people moving as in slow motion. Nurses removed catheters and tubes, even gently removed adhesive tape from Marna's face with alcohol before placing her in my arms.

The anxious and uncomfortable faces of nurses and one young doctor in the room blurred, and all I could see, all I could feel, was the cold and limp child in my arms. A bleeding ulcer had taken her life, but at that moment when I held her for the last time, all I could think was *This can't be true. I did not have this child for such an ending.* "Why? Oh, why do we have children? For this?" I cried out to the sad-faced doctor who only moments before had held a flashlight to Marna's pupils.

She could not answer and left the room quickly to warn Larry, who was coming back upstairs from the cafeteria with some soup for me.

As I held Marna, I realized that this was the first time in days that she had been freed of I.V. tubing, catheters, respirators, that her arms were finally released from the adhesive taping them to boards or bed. I hugged her, rocking slowly back and forth, comforting myself in the way I had formerly comforted my beautiful child. I was dumb with disbelief. Surely all those years of struggle could not be over now.

It seemed that as I held her there, loving her, I could still hear and feel the echo of rapid speech from her nurses, could still sense the bustle of frantic activity that had surrounded her only moments before. It was as though the sounds and frenzy still continued somewhere around me, but there was also a new and sickening silence. Larry and I held each other and Marna close together for the last time. I could not let go of this wonderful child I had come to love more than life itself.

I remember walking across the parking lot to our car that day, wondering how the sun could still shine. Even after all these years, I am afraid of the force of grief when I think about her and her last few days of life. On that ordinary June day, my youngest child died in my arms, and I continued, walled-in by my agony, for some time to come.

I would gladly have offered up my eyes, my hands, in

exchange for her life. After her death, I sometimes had to park my car a block or so from home, for privacy or to protect my other children, wanting to spare them the agony of seeing me cry, and I would scream at the God who allowed such injustice, such misery.

I wrote countless pages of fevered, indecipherable poetry, learning that there are no words adequate to describe the death of a beloved child.

The one thing I had always believed from the birth of my very first baby was that I would not be able to live through the sorrow of ever losing one of my children. I was sure that the trauma of losing a child was beyond my powers of coping.

For months thereafter I might be shopping or driving somewhere and suddenly be startled into thinking I "saw" Marna walking with a stranger or riding in the back seat of a car. I guess I kept looking for her, part of my mind still refusing to believe that she was really gone.

I would awaken suddenly in the middle of the night, believing I heard her familiar coughing, and perhaps even jump to my feet to assist her. I struggled to conceal my suffering from my family, hoping to protect them from its intensity. The pent-up sorrow made me implode with pain, emotional and physical; the migraines now controlled my daily life. Writing her book—her life story—and joining other parents as volunteers to raise funds for research into cystic fibrosis became my therapy. The same energy and commitment I had utilized to care for Marna was now channeled into another kind of fight against the disorder that had claimed her.

Larry's grief, although overwhelming at first, did not last as long as mine, and he began to function soon after her death. When we left the hospital on that last day's visit, however, we had planned to go directly to his mother's home a few short miles away. It had been Larry's home all of his childhood, too, so when in his confusion and grief he became lost and could not find his way, the symbolism was hard to overlook.

To my amazement, I still managed to walk and breathe. I even tried to teach my piano students within a couple of weeks of Marna's death, yet life seemed unreal, dreamlike and hazy in spite of returning routines that should have helped me.

Larry's love was not enough to sustain me, nor was my own love for him and my children. Something deep inside me was forever changed, and when I looked into the mirror I saw an expression in my eyes that was to remain there permanently. No matter how I might smile or laugh in the future, there would always be that expression of deep, inconsolable sadness in the eyes, like a password that anyone who had undergone such loss could recognize immediately.

I learned so many things from her passing out of my life. I discovered that when a parent's primary concern deals with the life of a child who requires special treatment, something has to fill the void when that care is no longer needed. The actual struggle to keep her well and alive created its particular place in my daily schedule, and instead of relief when that ceased to be necessary, I felt a total disorientation. I was lost, in the truest sense of the word.

The blessed numbness that sets in to protect us following such an experience only lasts a couple of weeks at best, and just when relatives and friends return to their own lives and activities, it wears off for the bereaved. Antidepressants and other drugs only prolong the inevitable. One must cope and deal with the reality of the loss.

I also learned that all of those things that I had formerly

derided—such as taking flowers to the cemetery, for example—I now made part of my new ritual. My common sense told me that she was not "there" in that cemetery, but in my grief I kept returning to her grave site as if looking for her. This behavior would have seemed bizarre to me before, but now it was essential.

Most surprising was the tremendous guilt I felt. I later learned that it is not at all unusual for a parent to experience this when a child dies. Since our children are not supposed to precede us in death, when they do, it strikes deeply into our subconscious: Somehow we must have failed to supply the protection they required.

Sensitive that Diep saw death and witnessed children die regularly in her war-torn world, I said little to her about my loss.

Dear Diep,

Our Marna died two weeks ago, and I have not been feeling well. This accounts for the fact that you haven't heard from me for a time.

I'm sending you some clothes for the children. There are some things which were Marna's and which I know your babies can wear. . . .

Her response was immediate.

Dearest Sister,

Marna was so little, so cute. I'm so sorry about your little girl. We love our children and they are a part of us. Nothing can replace. It is the same for any real mother, no matter how or where. A child dies, and something dies too inside the mother forever.

Diep

Something had, indeed, died within me, but something had been gained as well. Unwillingly, I now had membership in that sorority of which so many Vietnamese mothers were members.

I still lived in daily pain, suffering from headaches to the point where at times I was nearly suicidal.

"If you continue with that book you started about Marna two years ago, I think that the writing will be valuable therapy for you," her doctor told me one afternoon on the phone.

"But that was a happy, optimistic book, a book about the experience of having a beautiful little girl who just happened to have cystic fibrosis," I protested. "It was a care-and-maintenance book, intended to inspire and encourage other C/F parents. Now that she's dead . . ."

"There are still thousands and thousands of C/F parents with children fighting Marna's fight," he said gently. "Your book can be a book about her love of life. It need not be a book just about her death!"

I went to work on my book, *Child in White Fog*. Near the book's conclusion I wrote:

When a little time has passed, giving me more distance, a different perspective, it will be time to probe this throbbing pain in my search for some answer to it all. Perhaps then I could make her death, but especially her life, meaningful to someone else, somewhere. There must be a viable translation to this agony, hers which has just ended and mine which goes on. By putting it down on paper, I seek to transcend human mourning, as our Marni emerged triumphantly. For me, writing it down becomes just a slower verbalization, requiring an organization of thought made chaotic by grief. It necessitates a seeking out of answers.

Larry had known months and months of watching me go through this relentless suffering, and he hated the effect the drugs had on my personality. When I was pain-free, I seemed to tiptoe or glide through life, not really connecting with reality, only making a pass at those activities that demanded anything of me. When I was drug-free, I was emotional, suffering, nauseated, and generally incapacitated, wondering why the pain wasn't fatal and wishing it were.

Although at the time it was a nightmare, the afternoon when I went to tutor a high-school student and couldn't drive home because of the near paralysis in my neck and back was really the beginning of my salvation. It was clear now that I had to have surgery to fuse the discs ruptured in the accident.

The first of three separate cervical fusion operations took place in February 1970. I remember the doctors telling me the night before that four cervical discs were ruptured, and I remember wishing I'd die under the anesthetic and then crying Marna's name over and over when I came to in the recovery room.

In the back of my mind lurked a fear I could not voice: My marriage to Larry was in jeopardy. The financial struggles, the trauma of losing Marna following three years of caring for her and administering her therapy, the stresses of rearing the other four, and my injury and health problems had taken their toll on Larry. He tried valiantly to cope, but I often saw his facade crumble when he thought I wasn't watching.

Perhaps the hardest things for him to deal with were "my absences," as he called them—times when I was so zapped on painkillers that I couldn't even experience the normal happy moments life had to offer. He felt abandoned, at times even hopeless.

Although a whole year had passed since Marna LeAnn's death, my recovery was far from complete. I lacked the wisdom to seek professional help, thus relying upon myself to pull out of the depression and pain, a pain whose source was often unclear. Was it physical, a result of the injury I had sustained in the accident, or emotional, caused by the death of my child?

Sometimes when I took a shot for pain, I was unclear as to where I hurt. Everywhere? The suffering was so total that I wasn't sure. The way one's body comes to tolerate toxins is amazing, and soon I was giving myself several shots or more a day and still functioning so well that no one realized it.

I wasn't always rational or functioning so well, however. There were nightmare situations in my life in those days that make me shudder to recall now. One evening in particular comes to mind. After having had several shots throughout the day, I had words with Larry and took off in the car. I arrived at a busy and popular restaurant in town and wandered over to a table occupied by three men who were somewhere in their late twenties or early thirties.

"Can we buy you a drink or something?" one of them asked me. I shook my head. Their faces kept blurring. I remember being dazed, confused, as if in a trance. Nothing felt real. I just wasn't able to connect with anything, and I had moments when I wasn't even sure where I was.

The men tried to engage me in conversation, and one of them suggested that I shouldn't be driving. I must have looked as nauseated as I was feeling.

"Why don't you let us drive you home?" one of them offered. I might have taken this as a thoughtful gesture, but fortunately for me there was something in his expression that slipped through my Demerol haze. The men exchanged glances, thinking I was too far gone to recognize what was going on, and I began to sober up rather quickly. I started to get up, and one of them reached up and pulled me down into the chair. I was too weak to resist.

Fear and confusion took over, and I started to cry. How did I get here? What was I doing with these men, anyhow? Then I remembered. Marna was here somewhere. Did someone tell me that? How did I find this out? I had to find her before it was too late.

"My little girl . . . she's here somewhere," I said in a dreamy and tearful voice. I could hear my voice as if it came from somewhere else.

The men looked startled. For a moment, reality surfaced for me. "Your little girl?" one of them questioned.

"Yes, she's lost here . . . *I'm* lost . . . I don't know."

I was aware of them looking at each other strangely, then at me, and saying nothing. I started to get up once again. I was sure that I'd lost Marna in this crowd of people. She would never have wandered off like that. I believe that I started to sob.

"What . . . does your little girl look like?" The man was smiling broadly, ridicule and disbelief evident in his face and voice.

"I'm not . . . she . . . *she's dead!*" I said matter-of-factly.

The three men got up, grabbing their bill, and left promptly. In that moment, their nervousness came through to me clearly although I do not remember driving home later.

Perhaps the most frightening effect of the drug was the

amnesia that I experienced. I would awaken from a
Demerol-induced sleep, wander around the house not
knowing whether it was daytime or night, and try to discover from Larry just exactly what I had done immediately
after my last injection. I would try to be as clever as possible in my questioning so he wouldn't realize that I actually could not remember. Perhaps if he told me, I might
remember, yet I was always frightened that I would learn
some embarrassing or terrible truth about something I had
said or done. Usually my Demerol daze made me do silly
and mindless things; I would be caught up in some frantic
activity, something that seemed critically important to my
pain-weary mind.

One morning, Larry gave me an eyewitness account of
one of my "blackout" evenings. "You must have had a
shot last night before you finally collapsed in bed around
midnight, 'cause you decided to clean out the medicine
cabinet, spilling everying you touched into the sink. I tried
to coax you back to bed, but you wouldn't have it. Instead,
you began putting the contents of the medicine cabinet in
a paper bag, saying you'd take it to Safeway in the morning
for a refund."

This was the kind of craziness that made my heart pound
when he related it to me. Often I'd get a hazy picture of
the activity in my mind as he described it, but nothing was
clear or made any sense.

"You know," Larry told me, "for someone who is usually so bright, so alert and outgoing, the person you become after one of those damned shots is a complete
stranger. I married a vibrant, happy, very intelligent girl,
and you've become a zombie!"

He was right. The drug that was insulating me from
pain and suffering most of the time was also keeping from
me the sunlight and fresh air, even the fragrance of the

night-blooming jasmine twining on the lattice of our front porch. In order to block out the hurt, I also had to block out all the rest of life, too, and this was surely out of character for someone who had always wanted to experience life fully. Now life was a haze in which my feet never seemed to connect with anything.

When Larry and I were in public, he often had to hold my arm tightly if some little girl who even vaguely resembled Marna happened to pass by. Even when I had not had any medication, the confusion and aching for my child were so acute that I'd wander away, following some stranger's child, and Larry would have to pull me back gently.

"You get that lost, dazed look in your eyes," he would tell me, "and I get worried. Some day a mother's going to call the police on you, saying you're trying to kidnap her kid." He was only half joking.

One beautiful March day I went to pick camellias in the back yard, from the very camellia tree where Marna had posed for her last birthday photograph. Suddenly the tears began flowing and I realized that every day might produce something to trigger that misery, that longing, that defiance I felt against the inevitable and unchangeable.

"I must accept what *is*," I told myself aloud. "I have to live, and I'm not actually *living* when I have drugs in my system. I've simply got to find another way to control my pain!" There was only one thing I could think of to do. I rushed inside and located my last box of hypodermic needles containing the drug that had so controlled me, and with a shovel I dug a deep hole under the crab apple tree and buried the box. My survival instincts prompted me to symbolically remove my addiction, in the naive hope I could take whatever came my way.

The sad ending to this story will be familiar to anyone who has ever dealt with addiction. Several days later, I awoke with a blinding migraine. The agony pounded behind my left eye, and I could not find relief. I pressed ice packs to my head. I hid in the dark beneath the covers, with the windows draped and the bedroom as dark as possible. I made frequent trips to the bathroom to dry-heave, each spasm driving the sharp pain deeper into my head. I cried out in misery, and even the sound of my own voice made the pain worse.

Finally, desperate and blind with suffering, I braved the spring rain that poured down heavily outside and tried to find the shovel. In my disorientation and utter confusion, I could not find it, so I fell to my knees in the mud beneath the crab apple tree and clawed with my hands, attempting to uncover the box of painkillers to find relief. But it was not there. Had I buried it on the other side of the tree? I wept, the throbbing in my head unbearable now.

I frantically clawed and dug, breaking fingernails and hurting my fingers, but still no luck. Nearly hysterical with the terror that the migraine always produced, I dug more frantically than ever, searching for the blessed oblivion that lay there somewhere beneath the earth. It was useless. I could not find it.

"Oh, my God, is this the life I've chosen for myself?" I sobbed. "Will I ever be free from this torture?" Now I couldn't escape the suffering, and face down in the mud and rain, I sobbed, beaten and submissive, until Larry came and helped me up. He led me, exhausted and covered with mud, into the house, where I bathed and fell into bed.

I don't know exactly when or how it came about, but during the period following my third cervical fusion operation I made a decision to get well for good. Philosophically I had always rejected "drug therapy." The whole idea flew in the face of everything I believed about embracing life and learning from the blows. I had temporarily found the blows too much to bear, but I had also discovered that one cannot escape. Sooner or later you have to face your demons.

It would have been so much easier if we could have afforded a professional therapist. I never even considered looking for someone in one of those agencies that provide help for people in trouble who are also broke. Instead, I decided to just "tough it out," and tough it out I did.

I had read somewhere that following a severe loss, a truly healthy, balanced person might undergo a period of instability but would one day probably wake up and have the certain knowledge that the period had passed. It would be as if a great load had been lifted, and with that relief would come the awareness that it was time to let go of past pain and begin anew.

Well, I decided, now it was time to fill up voids with news ideals, new pursuits. It was time to begin anew.

My wonderful children and husband provided the incentive, as did my many interests and goals. The letters from Vietnam also gave me courage to fight, to find other ways of dealing with the migraine pain when it attacked, for I knew that Diep was experiencing her own kind of suffering thousands of miles away. There was a strength, and undeniable courage, which came through her letters, and I knew that the same courage was still deep within me, too. I would call upon it, believe in it, and win this battle.

Diep's greetings were always warm, and when I read her letters I felt a closeness to her. It puzzled me how much I cared for this woman I might never meet in person. Our cultures and backgrounds were so different; Vietnam seemed so remote, so unreal to me. Yet Diep was always real, and I trusted her for her integrity and sincerity as I trusted very few people.

Dearest Sister Jannice,

. . . I think about Marna. I'm very sad and sorry that you lost your girl. She looked so cute and smart, so God got her early. I wish I could comfort you. . . . My own first daughter attends the girl school at Da Nang. She can almost read and write Vietnamese language. My little one is 2½ years old now and she will be three years soon. She doesn't make much trouble for me, so I can work overtime. I work at the library daytime and I teach at the U.S. Army Education Center nighttime for spoken Vietnamese and French language.

I like to teach. My sister is teacher at girl high school. . . . I'm very sad about my country in the war, but we can't avoid and God can't help, because people they like to fight. . . . Vietnamese very unlucky in this war. . . .

I have small gift for you and small one for Donice. Please you give Donice and say: from Diep. I think you are wonderful mother and you teach her becoming good person as you are.

I will always keep a special place in my heart and an honest affection for you and I hope you will always think of me as your Vietnamese sister. Say hello to your children and good regards to your husband.

From Vietnam, with love,
Diep

During the months of recuperation following my surgery (which took place at Christmastime in 1970), Larry was hired to illustrate a science book for a San Francisco publishing company. His early years of training as an artist would pay off at last. It finally looked as though he could phase out of the insurance business.

Now that I began to return to my life, I became more aware of Diep than ever. She wrote me of her conflicting feelings.

Dearest Sister Jannice,

My children are fine and enjoyed very much the toys and clothes you sent them. I'm very emotion about your kindness, and if there is some thing in Vietnam I send you please tell so I can do. . . . I would like to bring my children to U.S. and come see you and thank you for all kindness going to us over here. I don't know how to tell all my feelings, but I remember deeply that you are wonderful lady and good person in my life. I don't know what I can do. But I'll try to be good person and good mother as you. . . . Da Nang, Vietnam, is far thousands miles from you, and so small country, and there is me here praying to God bless you and love you same as an old sister. . . .

I know you worry lots about us here. There are my family sisters, brothers and old father who still need my help. Sometimes I look at my cute and naive children and cry to bring them to your free country. Then I look at my sisters and father, and I am so confused.

I don't work hard at the library and I don't take class at the Education Center now. My children would like me to be with them always, so now I only work at library daytime. . . . I send you pictures of us and you say good regards to your husband.

Diep

I wrote her back at once.

Dearest Sister Diep,

I can sympathize with your problem, and wish that I had an answer. I am so frightened for you, however. Now that our troops are being withdrawn from Vietnam, I fear that you will be in great danger. Having worked for the government and with two half-American children, your chances of surviving any Viet Cong takeover are not good. *Please* do what you can to get out. Make whatever arrangements you must and tell me how to help.

Jann

In none of her later letters did she ever mention why she procrastinated on seeking an exit visa. It would be many years before I would learn the real reason.

Her letters from Vietnam now contained pleas that I locate my ex-husband for her so that she could divorce him officially. I couldn't understand the urgency, although I had heard that in Vietnam she would be considered married while in the eyes of U.S. officials, my ex-husband probably was not. For some time, Diep had requested that I assist her, but by 1970 and early 1971 her letters had changed in tone from resignation over her situation to anxiety and then to raw fear.

"Do you suppose she's afraid now that the Communists will discover her marriage to an American, and that it will compound her danger?" I asked Larry one morning.

"It certainly is a liability for her," he said thoughtfully. "Look at the paper. It says that Australia and New Zealand have declared that they will withdraw their troops from South Vietnam. South Korea has announced that it will withdraw most of its 48,000 troops, and Nixon promises that the U.S. will pull out 45,000 men during December and January of 1972. The ramifications of this for the South Vietnamese could be pretty bad."

* * *

By the summer of 1972 I had completed all of my course work for a master's degree in English literature. A bachelor's degree in creative writing, along with some professional courses for teachers, were also behind me. Now all that loomed ahead was a written thesis, and once I found two readers who would be committed to my project, I thought I'd be set.

Never one to tackle simple tasks, I was determined to submit my thesis long before the deadline, which was hardly a reasonable goal. That meant that I would do the actual writing—the first and final draft—in two weeks! My subject was the impact and influence of Frieda Lawrence on the literature of her husband, D. H. Lawrence. Piles and piles of books lay on tables and the floor around my desk. I had read them all, but writing a book-length thesis with its strict requirements and format filled me with near terror.

The first afternoon that I tackled my typing chore was a disaster. The rule was that not more than three erasures could appear on one page. Not a very good typist—I'd put myself through college typing with four fingers—I continued to waste page after page of the also-required 75 percent rag-content paper. I could almost see dollar bills fluttering into my wastebasket with the crumpled-up paper that now filled it.

"I'll fix dinner," my daughter Donice offered. I accepted gratefully, then locked myself in my den and determined to get past this psychological block.

"Why don't you try a glass of wine. Relax," Larry suggested through the closed door. I told him that a glass of wine would really fix me: I'd probably fall asleep on the typewriter.

"I hear Hemingway swore by it," he said. "There were a few other . . ."

"Literary lushes?" I asked. He laughed and went away. In a few minutes he knocked on the door, and there he was with a glass of wine in hand. All else had failed, so I accepted. The result was that I soon adopted a what-the-heck attitude about it all, and I wrote the first few pages of my paper without any glaring errors.

One day I found Dottie on my front porch with a dazed look that made me think at first she had had a stroke. She didn't respond when I spoke to her, and as I led her into the house I was aware of her stiffened body, as though she were resisting some raging wind that might carry her away. Frightened, I kept saying her name over and over.

She held a pack of cigarettes tightly in her hand, almost crushing them, and stared at me vacantly with that lack of recognition one sees in the eyes of the severely mentally ill. Suddenly she threw herself into my arms.

"Scotty! It's Scotty! He . . . he's been killed! . . ."

Her beloved nephew had died in Vietnam, and she had just learned that his body was being sent home. She had received the shock all alone: Randy was out of town on a business trip, out of reach until evening. I comforted her as best I could, feeling shocked when I discovered that Scotty had been killed in Da Nang.

The realization that Scotty had died in Diep's own town brought the situation there more in focus for me. During the past two years part of my mind had continued to deny that Diep herself was in mortal danger, even though I knew better. I was aware of her plight but managed to put it out of my mind much of the time, reasoning that I could drive myself crazy worrying about something that I was helpless to do anything about.

But there was always that nagging doubt: Was there really nothing I could do? With Scotty's death I resolved to intensify my letter-writing campaign to help Diep leave Vietnam. I'd heard that there were ways of getting her out of Vietnam, and was convinced that once she saw the certainty of Da Nang's fall she would choose to leave.

Public opinion in the United States had dictated President Nixon's withdrawal plan, although there never was any clear-cut schedule. The My Lai massacre, a nonhealing wound for the war-weary American people, had fueled a wave of antiwar feeling, and the evening news devoted considerable time to its depiction. With the My Lai tragedy, I came to realize, as did millions of others, what can happen to decent human beings in war, and how the savage who knows no compassion is near the surface in many people, waiting to be tapped. As it turned out, the senseless murder of 347 women, old men, and children at My Lai was far from a unique incident.

Although my daily routine of mundane chores and the goals I drove myself to meet, helped distract me from becoming absorbed in the war, Diep's letters kept me conscious of the war most of the time. When I wasn't writing to her or sending her some small, useful gifts, I was thinking about her and her two little girls in a country that was being virtually destroyed. I had long before resolved that if it were ever possible, I would try to help Diep and her daughters. This became a quiet goal, an idea that never left me.

"I know why she continues to write to you," Dottie said one morning over coffee. "What I can't figure out is why you keep up what must be an aggravating correspondence with her. You've asked her again and again to make arrangements in Vietnam to leave, and her letters show that she's fully aware of the situation. So how come you continue to hope that she will make a move to save herself when she obviously wants to stay right where she is?''

"I don't think she truly believes that Vietnam will fall," I told Dottie. "There'll be a phrase here or a sentence there that is heartbreaking, showing she knows her danger, and then she'll talk about the spring flowers or the coming new year. I just can't figure it out."

"Hasn't Vietnam known something like a hundred years of war with someone or other?" Dottie asked.

"Meaning?"

"Well, when war is all you've ever known, and you've managed to live through it to adulthood, maybe you get a feeling of immortality or something," she said.

By now, I was ready to take action. In December of 1972, Larry and I took a "letter of promise" to be notarized. It read in part: ". . . [we] will be responsible for the shelter and lodging as sponsors of Nguyen Thi Diep, Nguyen Mai-Cat, and Nguyen Thi Mai-Uyen . . . [who] will be assured of never having to depend upon public assistance." The note went on to state our income, the fact that we owned our home, and other pertinent information. I had been advised at the San Francisco Vietnam Consulate that by sending copies of this to Diep, but especially to officials at the ODP (Orderly Departure Program) or the equivalent Catholic Relief offices, she might more easily be granted permission to leave Vietnam and come to the United States.

Everyone I asked had different advice. No one seemed to really know what procedures I should follow or to whom I might write and get the best results.

Dearest Sister,
    You said two boxes were sent me over here. I worry

about them because until today I did not receive yet, so I write you short letter let you know. We are fine, the weather is warm this time.

I don't know the future of my country and I don't know what I can do. . . . My boss moved back to Saigon. . . . I'll tell my children about your kindness when they grow up. . . . Sister, I fear they never grow up. . . . My Vietnam sister she marry soon. Her fiancé will work at VN Embassy in U.S. maybe. Perhaps she will take my children over there so they can be safe from the war and have good school. That's all I wish now. . . . I say good regard to your husband and children and send my love.

Diep

This was the first time that Diep even suggested that she might find a way to send her children out of Vietnam. My curiosity was piqued that she had not indicated greater concern before this. Then a letter came that told me she had at last found my ex-husband—and hers—and that he had remarried in the United States. Diep said the thing that had hurt her the most deeply was when he told her that he would bring *her* here but that she would have to give her children away first. Then he told her that he would pay her way, but that she would have to raise the money for her children's tickets. That had been eighteen months before, she said, but she was still reeling from it.

"Well," Larry said, "it's obvious he saw that as a way out of the relationship, knowing full well she'd never go along with it, and that there was no way she could raise that kind of money."

"Her letter says he told her that he still loves her; she's very bitter."

"I don't blame her. Americans bandy that word about freely, but perhaps the Vietnamese don't. In any event, she's a grown woman and should know enough stories about abandoned Vietnamese women to fill volumes. I suspect those girls over there don't get involved with American servicemen without some understanding that 'forever' only means a weekend, or at best a short visit.''

Another letter arrived, and this time Diep's fear was unmistakable.

> . . . I just worried about the rockets . . . very dangerous to live here . . . but it seems too late for my decision now. Vietnamese police station did not give any order to get out the country this time. My children are so afraid the rockets and the death. They see the death all around and wait for it. . . . I'm very sad and the late week I lost everything too. Someone stole my TV and radio. I want to cry. . . . I will send you a handbag, very pretty. My new address will be in the Special Service Library at the U.S. Installation at Marble Mountain, so I can still send you the letters free.
>
> Diep

A photo in *Time* magazine showed a column of Vietnamese soldiers, ARVN troops, moving up the Dong Ha River. I was struck by their youth; some appeared to be barely in their teens. I wondered then if I might not have remained detached and basically oblivious to the war if Diep had not entered my life. I didn't think that would have been the case, but I couldn't be sure.

The most distressing letter of all came near the end of the year.

> Dearest Sister,
>
> I write you this letter to let you know we are O.K., but the air of the war is over my country and death is

hovering here. I don't know what will be, but I always
pray God save us. . . . My brother-in-law was killed in
Quang Ngai, and I was very sorrow and so painful, and
I still worry about my sister in Pleiku. Central Highland
is very bad over there. The city got off limit. I am very
confused. I know the war will take us now. Many people
all around no home, no food, and the death all around,
all around. I still work in the library, very dangerous
station, air field library near Marble Mountain. . . .
V.C. want to take this place. . . . I am so afraid.

My poor little girls they told me to send them to you
so they may live long life. They are afraid V.C. will cut
off the head. They see head cut off many times. I don't
know what to do, because I lost my decision to leave
and have no money. Do not sent money. It will be taken
and for nothing. . . . I will still send you a nice bag real
soon. Please give my regards. . . . All my loves from
us to you and your family.

Your sister in Vietnam,
Diep

This was followed a few weeks later by another letter:

. . . I remember myself when I was young girl, so
happy and carefree. Was it really true? I regret not loving that time more. . . . V.C. rockets come early in the
morning and someone died. God has forgotten Vietnam. . . .

. . . The rockets go overhead at night and we relief
when they miss. . . . My little girls so scared. I tried to
sell my home, but no one want. I cry when my little
girls want food and there is no food. . . . You are a
sister to me, perhaps more than a sister to me you are
so good. I never forget your kindness and loves going

to us here. My brother-in-law left wife and six children. He died in camp by the rocket, and they called my younger brothers now (17 and 18) and they say Emergency Station needs people. . . . Why this war so long? Why this war so long?

I mailed her a box of clothes of different sizes—men's, women's, and children's clothes that I had collected. I enclosed a plastic bottle of aspirin, as she had told me in previous letters how hard it was to get, as well as a bottle of vitamin C she had requested. In the box, I tucked two bags of hard candy for her children.

Later letters from Diep indicated that she never received the package.

After months of course work, study, and commuting, and an approved master's thesis, I was finally to receive my degree. The ceremony at San Francisco State University was quite long, and the children were bored and tired before it was over. All they knew was that I was relieved and happy, that I'd been working for this for a long time, and that now we could celebrate by having an ice cream sundae.

My former husband had apparently felt ambivalent all along about Larry adopting the children. Although there was no direct contact between the children and their father most of the time, and visits had been infrequent, Ed had difficulty really letting go. As a consequence, the divorce had not been friendly, and there had not been any contact between us since that time. We finally decided that adoption by Larry was the best solution for all concerned.

The children were each interviewed by the judge in Martinez, California. They were asked questions about their home life and about Larry and how they felt about him. When the adoption was officially granted, it felt as if we were getting married once again, only this time the children were six years older, and one of them was missing.

We celebrated our union with ice cream cones and laughter. Nothing was really changed since we had been a family all along, with the children choosing to call Larry "Dad," but everything seemed altered just the same. They now took his last name and they were allowed to change any part of their own names they wished to change, which was an exciting idea for two of them. Of course, this "bit of legality" assured Larry of his position within his family, a position he had accepted long ago, but, just the same, the formality of it made a psychological difference to us both.

After our ice cream cones, I took some flowers out to Marna LeAnn's grave to include her in our celebration. I sat there in the warm sun and talked to her for a few minutes. "You were always just like Larry's baby, Honey, from the first. We all know that, now and always."

Chapter Five

"Da Nang Is Gone.
I Shall Die Here!"

Dearest Sister,

Last week a man lives near had death by rocket. He was killed sleeping at night in bed when rocket went over us. My poor children wanted to see him one week later when his family could be found to come. My poor girls come home crying about the sight and smell. . . .

Although the syntax sometimes made her letters confusing, the powerful emotion always came through. So did the humor, which had much to do with my developing admiration for Diep. In spite of the horrors that were now an integral part of her life, she could still see the absurdity in some situations. She had the ability to laugh at the ironic and ridiculous, and she could find momentary joy in those few simple things that survived the devastation around Da Nang.

Despite her limited vocabulary, Diep was still capable

of conveying sadness, anxiety, joy and courage; Diep's letter might tell about death and destruction in her city, but carefully pressed flowers were often enclosed between its pages. There was never a complaining or whining tone to her letters. Her predominant fear was always for her children's safety, but the other tragedies she endured were accepted with a sad resignation, an acquiescence.

Diep had owned two houses during the midsixties. As the main provider for her brothers and sisters and her own children, she used the rental income from one house for support while she and her family occupied the other.

Her home, of which she was very proud, was a simple one-story brick-and-stucco building with asphalt tile floors and a well; it was located on the outskirts of Da Nang, about ten miles from the U.S. army base. Prior to 1970 her living conditions were comfortable. Her house was relatively modern and very neat, and it had the luxuries of a television set, a radio, and a tape recorder.

Very proud of her children, Diep always put them first. She took them to work with her when they were tiny, and because she feared that her superiors at the USO library would fire her if they knew she had her children with her at work, she sometimes managed to hide the girls under her desk. She often mentioned that they learned discipline from infancy on and "kept very still, not making any noise" when others were around.

The walk to the army bus, which took her to work every morning, was along the river. The descriptions in her earliest letters of those days prior to the departure of Jolie's father for the United States are idyllic. She was optimistic, never really believing that the war would change their lives any more than it already had. Before 1970, there was little talk about Americans withdrawing from Vietnam, and for

Diep the philosophies, values, and culture of the Western world had become an integral part of her life.

No one living in Vietnam could remember a time when there had not been war. The country's history is one of war and occupation. All through Diep's life there had been an uneasy awareness of and accommodation to war. To have never known a time when their country was not engaged in conflict would be inconceivable to Americans today, but for those in other countries, in which occupation or war has been the "norm," the horrors and responsibilities and even the inconveniences are kept in a kind of mental closet. It is a situation not unlike living in a small town whose chief industry is the paper mill, where the putrid odor of wood pulp is no longer noticed by the town's inhabitants but nearly asphyxiates the visitors.

Diep clung to her memories of serenity—or the closest semblance to it—and as a young adult she refused to relinquish the poetry and fantasies of her childhood. I often saw this in her letters and marveled at it. But I was also sometimes frustrated by the apparent naiveté or made frantic by her seeming inability to grasp the situation as I perceived it from the news coverage that I followed.

Between 1972 and 1973, however, her reactions changed. Her letters contained more references to the war and suffering, and I recognized her developing awareness that she might not survive after all. Her vacillation between optimism and resignation often left me perplexed. When a humorous anecdote was recounted on line four of her letter, followed by the description of a man being beheaded on line six, the incongruous parallel left me stunned.

There was one fact she did not disclose to me for a long time, or perhaps I did not understand it; and by the time it had come to light it was too late to act on. Diep's de-

termination—expressed through her constant request that
I help her locate my ex-husband—"to make papers of divorce" never seemed very important to me. I couldn't
understand why she was so eager to be legally free of
him. What difference did it make? I wondered. Even after
she wrote to me saying that she had finally heard from
him and that he had remarried in the U.S., her concern
about a legal divorce—where he would have to petition for
it—did not make much sense. It's *his* problem, I thought.
In Vietnam, with no visible husband, how could her life
be affected one way or the other?

What I didn't know was that her somewhat hasty marriage to my exhusband following months of no communication from Jolie's lieutenant-colonel father, had been a
mistake that was underscored when Diep finally received
word from that officer in the States: He had had a change
of heart; he wanted her at his side after all. There was a
good chance, she thought, that she could come to the States
and be at his side, as he offered to send for her and pay
her way. "I could not let him pay my way there when I
was another man's wife!" she was later to explain. "There
could be much trouble." Her reluctance to leave parents
and siblings was certainly a factor as well, but her marital
dilemma was the major problem.

I wrote to Congressman Jerome Waldie on her behalf in
July of 1972. Then I told Diep to encourage her.

Diep wrote to me in response:

Dear Mrs. Jannice,

I have your picture when you were 18. [He] left it
here. Well, I'm sending you the papers that say I was
his wife on the paper. Truth, I did not love him at first.
The employees at the club where Ed worked said that
because of me he come to see me and not pay attention

to his work, so when kitchen fire kill a man they blame Ed and fire him from job. They say it his responsibility to oversee things. He was sent to Qui Nhon. It is far away from Da Nang. That is the reason I made my decision to marry him and make papers for marriage, but later I learned he so changed I not be happy with him.

You say in late letter that you write Congressman Jerome Waldie. Maybe he grant me special favor and give my letter of introduction to the Consular in Da Nang? I become confused very much and get the headache. I am not the same as some Vietnamese women, Sister. I tried to keep the pure life of a mother, and we still live in the poverty situation. I want to work with my education for the money. I always try to be good person and lead my children in the right way of life.

Some ladies in the United States get their letters from their boyfriends over here and the letters written by me. The boys don't know how to read or write well, and they pay *me* to write their love letters. Very funny! They sometimes have the Vietnamese girl friends here in Da Nang, and they don't know how to read or write Vietnamese either. They have me write them. Then some Vietnamese girl friends from the country and don't have much education, and *they* don't know how to read and write. When they get to the U.S., I hope Americans don't think all Vietnamese ladies are the same.

She was still employed by the library in Da Nang. Her letter went on to say that Da Nang was ". . . calmer than other cities in South Vietnam, but we have many refugees in this small city; people from three cities come here to sell everything they own." They would bring tape recorders, radios, television sets, iceboxes, fans, ". . . but no one wanted to get. They worry about food. Not enough."

Rarely did a week pass that I wasn't either writing to

someone on Diep's behalf or thinking about her and her children. I wrote to the secretary of state, William Rogers, in Washington, D.C., and one day received the following letter:

Dear Mrs. Jansen:

I have received your letters and one dated July 27, 1972, from the Honorable Jerome R. Waldie, House of Representatives here in Washington, concerning the young Vietnamese woman, Diep, and her two little girls.

To be admitted into the United States, Diep and her children must have immigrant visas issued to them by an American consular officer abroad. She should, therefore, if she has not already done so, communicate with the Consular Section of the American Embassy at Saigon which will be glad to inform her of the requirements to be met and the procedure to be followed in her case. I am enclosing fact sheets about the requirements to be met by an applicant for an immigrant visa, the limitations on immigration, and the procedure to be followed to obtain a labor certification with the thought that you may wish to send them on to your friend in Vietnam. . . .

The letter went on to say that:

. . . Diep must obtain a labor certification based upon a job offer in the United States. The basic purpose of such a certification is, of course, to insure that employment opportunities are first made available to citizens and permanent residents of the United States.

Until Diep presents to the consular officer an approved labor certification based on a job offer in the

*United States, or satisfactory evidence that she is exempt
from that requirement, she cannot be registered for immigration. . . .*

The last few words made my heart pound. I suddenly
felt that helpless desperation that comes when one is caught
entangled in red tape. Frustrated, I wrote a letter to Waldie and Rogers once again, pointing out the difficulty in
helping Diep meet that job requirement and once again
pointing out her loyalty to our country and her precarious
situation. I also wrote to numerous other individuals—to
anyone I thought might offer information or assistance.
One of those was David M. Abshire, then the assistant
secretary for Congressional relations, who wrote to me on
March 10, 1973.

Nonpreference Vietnamese visa numbers are currently available for qualified applicants. . . . Therefore,
if Diep is found otherwise qualified for a visa, she should
experience no delay in the consideration of her case because of foreign state limitations of the law. Of course,
the easiest thing would be for her American husband to
assist her. . . .

I had learned that Ed had remarried, so any hope of
enlisting his help in bringing Diep to the States was remote. Furthermore, I had no desire to create problems for
his new wife, who might even be unaware of Diep's ex-
istence.

Abshire's letter went on to say:

The United States is withdrawing its troops from
Vietnam as the South Vietnamese become stronger and
more capable of defending themselves. We believe that

the government of Vietnam is able to offer far more protection for its citizens than might have been true in the past, and in any case we have no evidence to support the contention that the enemy is specifically targeting the thousands of Vietnamese who have worked with and for the United States.

The responsibility we feel for South Vietnam is directed toward all citizens of that country. As ample testimony to that responsibility, I cite more than 50,000 dead and the billions of dollars we have spent in helping the South Vietnamese to defend themselves from the invasion from the North.

The President is attempting to continue to fulfill our responsibility to South Vietnam by searching for a solution that will not only allow us to withdraw our troops in an honorable manner, but also will bring the killing to a halt. The missing ingredient in this solution is that which has been missing all along, namely the cooperation of the men in Hanoi.

Diep had just informed me that she had taken another Amerasian child into her home to care for, a boy whose mother was too poor to feed him. Diep was still working part-time for our army in a base library, so she had some financial assistance. Also, as long as she was employed there, her letters could be mailed without expense to her.

Diep wrote her own letters to U.S. congressmen. Here is one letter she sent to Jerome Waldie, then representing the 14th District in California.

Dear Sir:

I am Vietnamese lady and I hope that this letter will reach you soon. I am confident in your help and kindness. Will you please give me a special favor as follows:

I had worked for the United States government in almost 10 years as a librarian of the USARVN Special Services Library agency. I can type, write, read, file, and translate in English, and I have a senior high-school degree and studied correspondence course Library Science A-54 (Organization of Library materials) from the University of Wisconsin.

I need a job very much to support my three children. They are two girls and an adopted boy of the Vietnamese and American blood. They are very smart and cute. They always kept high grade in their classes. Sir, I have always tried to be good mother about material and spiritual life for them. We live in the poor condition in this material society. I kept the pure life of a mother. Their father had returned to the Unites States as of 1968. After three years in Vietnam he had got married to American lady, and I couldn't make the papers to come to the United States. I did not ask any help of him after his marriage. I would keep his family in happy and his position out of trouble. I think he cares for his officer life, and he is a high officer now. I know where he is, but I did not write him, although I still love him very much and couldn't forget him.

I know you are a good person and kind. Please help and pity this lady, sir, and will give me a special favor letter to introduce me to the Consular and USAID in Da Nang; maybe I get job with my education to take care of my three sweet, naive children that they may have better life and continue their school. I think that your letter will help me much and your kindness are same as God blessing us in the material and spiritual life. I hope to hear from you soon. I truly appreciate and thank you very much for any help on your part.

Respectfully yours,
Nguyen Thi Diep

Waldie, in turn, contacted Secretary of State Rogers:

June 11, 1973
Hon. William Rogers
Secretary of State
Department of State
Washington, D.C.

Dear Mr. Secretary:

We have had previous correspondence with the State Department in regards to the desires of Nguyen Thi Diep to obtain entrance to the United States, and I call your attention to letters dated August 15, 1971, November 12, 1971, March 10, 1972, and January 4, 1973, (copies) addressed to me. Your letter to Mrs. Jansen and the one to me dated March 10, 1973, advised that Diep's entrance into this country is not possible under present circumstances.

Since then, I have had letters from Diep and her friend Mrs. Jansen, my constituent, relative to the possibility of employment with the American Consulate in Da Nang, or any other office under American jurisdiction— these documents are enclosed for your consideration.

In view of all the facts in this case, and my sympathy for Diep and her plight, I should appreciate anything you can do to help her at this time. May I hear from you at your earliest convenience?

Sincerely yours,
Jerome R. Waldie, M.C.

And so it went, with letter upon letter between Diep and me, between Diep—in care of me—to officials here in the United States, and letters from me to the same officials. When the replies came after weeks or months, the news or advice was never encouraging.

Dottie tried to comfort me. "She is not your responsibility. You can only do your best, but it's not as though you don't have enough on your mind. Why, sometimes I think you just like to keep yourself in stress, as though you thrive on it.''

She didn't mean to be unkind, I realized, but Dottie just couldn't understand why I felt such a commitment to some woman I'd never seen and probably never would.

''Hey, she's just one of millions,'' Dottie would chide. ''You want to be a do-gooder? There are enough people in this county alone who could use a handout, you know. So why spend time spinning your wheels over a woman in Vietnam who's no worse off than most of her countrymen, and who is probably going to do just fine once the war's over?''

''If she can find a lonely serviceman with no ties in the States,'' Randy chimed in, ''she'll quickly forget her pen pal in California.'' He winked good-naturedly, but his irritation with me was evident in his voice.

In the meantime, ''Vietnamization'' was winning popular support in this country because it meant that we were bringing our American servicemen home at last. It was also a clear indication that—for this country at least—the war was ending. Our policy of disengagement might have soothed politicians and citizens alike, but to expect that the South Vietnamese would be able to really hold their own after our departure was ludicrously naive. I doubted then that anyone really believed that we were ''strengthening South Vietnam's government and armed forces.'' That was certainly the intention, but time has shown that this was an unrealistic expectation. As might be expected, the North Vietnamese stepped up their infiltration into the south with our Vietnamization program. When the news media pointed out that in order to counter the Communist build-up, our bombers had attacked enemy supply dumps and all the routes in Laos and the northwest corner of

South Vietnam, it provoked, of course, antiwar groups into a frenzy that was recorded on television wherever possible.

While Nixon insisted he was winding down our involvement and providing the South Vietnamese with the training and supplies to fight their own war, peace-movement leaders in this country accused the administration of duplicity, asserting that the fighting had actually increased. However, most of the casualties were now Asian rather than American.

Diep felt dual loyalties. Although she had sometimes felt more American than Vietnamese, she was proud of her heritage and background. Her letters depicted a woman who genuinely loved her own country yet yearned for the freedom and opportunity in the United States. The birth of her daughters had augmented her desire to come here, simply because she wanted the best for them, and "the best" in her thinking began and ended with a good education.

As the Americans began leaving Vietnam, the changing attitudes toward the children they left behind were beginning to be felt more keenly. The Vietnamese had never accepted the mix of Caucasian and Asian to begin with, but the Communists were to make it harder on the Amerasian youngsters and their mothers "of divided loyalty." From Diep's letters, I learned about her deep love for children, and of her anguish particularly over the suffering of Vietnam's children, which she was compelled to witness every day. As the mother of two Amerasian children, Diep already faced some derision and alienation from her community, but when she reached out to help other half-American babies, her risk of calling attention to herself with the V.C. sympathizers was increased. She knew it, too. The little boy adopted by Diep was not only the child of a poverty-stricken mother; he was also a "fear child," a child whose mother feared to acknowledge him.

Diep often wrote about such children. The abandoned young of abandoned mothers, they were not claimed by either country and virtually lived in the streets—subhuman with animalistic cunning, sometimes treacherous, always hungry, angry, and desperate. Diep knew she had to stay alive to protect her beloved babies from such a fate. Her children were her reason for living—often her *only* reason for choosing life.

She expressed her conflicts to me.

Dearest Sister,

How are you doing this time? Jeanie had to stay home from school. Her school now used for refugees' home. Da Nang is very hot this time. Sister, you understand I want to come to U.S., but don't have money for trip even to Saigon, and it is not safe to send money for me through mail now. Won't receive. Sometimes I think about my children's future and mine, and see only the darkness before my eyes. I would be so sad to leave my beautiful country and family here, but if V.C. win I can't live with the V.C. government. I'm very confused. I work here just enough to buy the food, and don't have enough food for all. I could have the American boy-friend and then have much money for my children, but now my mind won't do that. I have to live for my children's spiritual life, not for myself. If I take the American boyfriend now, my pure children ask questions I would be ashamed to answer. I have to respect their young souls and their naive hearts. I have to be good for them.

Some servicemen say the ARVN strong and can win against the V.C. You think so? Some say that Americans go home so that V.C. not be cruel to South Vietnam people. If later you help me to leave here, I'll try to work to pay you when I go to work over there. I don't like to take advantage of your kindness and your niceness to us. Thank you very much.

I never forget your good heart and I never find the second one. You are sweet as a real sister to me, and maybe sweeter than a real sister.

Well, once again I try to sell my home. No one want. The war made me lose much money. If we can get to you, we don't eat much food. We not eat much and don't cause you troubles. I can do any job and will do. I clean for you or make anything.

Diep

Her refusal to accept what seemed inevitable made me angry one moment and sorrowful the next. Vietnam would surely fall. Ed's statement that there would be a bloodbath stuck in my mind. From what I read and saw on television, it seemed likely. I wondered sometimes if Diep's resigned desperation, her acceptance of the tragic, was real. I wondered, too, if her sense of humor, sometimes so incongruous, was genuine or just my interpretation? Did she really possess the stability, the quiet strength that accepted what she could not change while she struggled to win what lay within her power?

One letter contained a clear cry for help.

Dearest Sister,

You are my sweet hope for some life for my cute little girls. For me it no matter much, but they are my breath, my life. Without them, there is no breath in this body, but I must see to save them.

I have sad story to tell you. Someone they take my

TV and radio and other things, and they take all my money, too. The V.C. is behind this terrible thing that happened to me, I think. I have no money, but do not send me some, because they take it away before I receive. I do not know what to do now. I feel as little as a blade of grass in the monsoon rains. Some soldiers they give me their C rations, and this is good for my children. Beans and franks and limas [beans?] and ham, and some sweet fruit called the apricot with juice.

In the night it is green-gold, a bad dream in the dark, when the flares and rockets go off. The V.C. they only attack after midnight, late in the darkness, and they are like shadows of death and treachry [sic] as they hurt our ears with the machine guns and they make the ground shake and tremble. My poor babies, they so afraid. Oh, Sister, help me if you can.

Diep

"Please fill out the green slip," the postal clerk directed. It was a familiar procedure now, since I frequently packaged and mailed yarn, clothing, vitamins, and aspirin to Diep. As I checked off "gift" in the appropriate box, I also itemized the contents of the package: "aspirin, Ben-Gay (she had asked for this by name), candy, vitamin C . . ."

"I'm sorry," the clerk said apologetically, "but there is a new list of restrictions." He produced a thick book and ran a finger down long columns until it came to rest on "No drugs . . . food . . ." I took Diep's package home.

On my dresser was a recent letter in which Diep had described taking her little girls to the orphanage near the airfield, where "Baby Airlift" planes were ready to take children the following morning to the United States. She told about how they had all cried together when she left them there, her children's tear-streaked faces vivid in her mind as she made her way home without them. Then she described how, just before dawn, when she feared it might be too late, she made the hasty, heart-pounding journey back again and frantically retrieved her daughters.

It was a decision loaded with guilt: Was she committing them to future deprivation, perhaps even suffering and torture? Was she denying them the freedom, the education, the very *life* they deserved, merely because she could not bear to part with them?

That anguished trip to the airfield was not the last one of its kind for Diep. The tearful scene was repeated at least one more time, and her final decision then, too, was to bring Jeanie and Jolie back home with her. Was it her hope and optimism that won over her fear for her children's safety? Or was it that they were too precious to let go, representing her very breath, her only reason for breathing? Perhaps her eleventh-hour change of mind in each case was a little of both—optimism *and* her adoration for her babies.

Her world was beginning to collapse, as her letters revealed.

Dearest Sister,

I hope my letters coming to you and we are confident in your kindness. Sometimes your letters opened and I know they read before I get them.

Please understand my situation this time. We are now refugees of this war. Some V.C. took our things and I cried. I felt so bad, but no good. If V.C. stay here, we must die. They will cut off our heads the same way they do friends in Da Nang. It is easy to die in this time.

I don't have any papers to show them to get to the U.S. Do you still have copies of our birth certificates that you returned? We have nothing. I don't even have courage enough to give my children away when I don't know what will happen to them.

Dear Sister, if the war comes very fast now, will you take my children if they get out? Please adopt my poor children. They sweet and not cause you trouble. Please just make them safe for me. Then later you can find someone else to adopt them.

I think truly that I die anyway. . . .

A letter from Diep's sister Minh, in Saigon, explained that Diep was very ill. She had a severe cough, had turned yellow; the doctor had advised immediate surgery. Minh pleaded that I send something to help pay for the operation Diep needed; she was unable to work, could barely walk, and couldn't keep any food down.

"You can send her money," advised the postal clerk, "but there's no guarantee that she'll ever receive it." I had only $56 in my checking account, so I sent a money order for $50 which Diep never received; the letter was delivered without it.

I've been very sick. I don't have operation because no money, but terrible sick. They cannot fix what I was sick about, something in my stomach out. I couldn't eat much. If I have enough to eat, hurt inside and when I walk I feel much hurt too. I don't know how to be better without operation. They say I must take a long time to rest. My finance in trouble.

My sister said you wrote me. Thank you for your true kindness and your loves going to me. You are the kindest person in my life.

Diep

Dear Diep,

I sent you money. Apparently you did not receive it. Please don't give up hope. Please continue to do what you can to leave Vietnam. We will do whatever we can to help you.

It hurts me to think that you have given up. You must come *with* your girls when the time is right, and they need you as their mother with them. Of course I would adopt them, if it came to that, but do not worry about them being abandoned. Please just get well.

Jann

A *Time* article with its color photographs of the war lay open on my coffee table, showing a full-page picture of three infants, nearly naked and without shoes, huddled against the cold and rain. In the wide and frightened eyes of those Vietnamese babies I saw my Marna in the last hours before her death. It was an expression I was to remember all the days of my life, and the helplessness I felt in that hospital room that June afternoon was the helplessness I was now feeling with regularity where Diep was concerned.

Her fear was evident in a letter sent on November 18, 1974.

Dear Mrs. Jannice,

I want to cry for my country. I couldn't write you sooner. Millions of us. We don't like the V.C., but we don't know where we can go if they come here with Communist government. I hope you like the handbag. It made by the hand, of bamboo.

Diep

Ten days later, she wrote again.

Dear Sister,

   . . . I will die. I don't have any way to leave now. No money for transportation from here to other city. If I leave here we will be hungry and get sick. I saw many painful people over here. They sit on street, no home, no food. If V.C. comes here, we will have to move, and we will be the same. I cried and could not sleep when I saw my poor children. Maybe we will die . . . everyone try to live here . . . the war air is covered with fire and rockets . . . many children got missing . . . when the V.C. mortared the city, the children no clothes, no money, no food. . . . Some family they have five children, but when they get here they were missing two. It is so sad situation. I work just few days but not get paid yet. If I get paid, I send you something nice. Every day I go to work I cried when seeing many people hungry. I have to give them 15¢ for to buy one bread. I give the people the clothes of my children and mine too, and every day people go around and ask every house for some rice for one meal. We are very hurt inside. Just the rich have a way to avoid the painfulness of war. . . . Some mothers come here carrying babies who died, but when they walked for miles and many miles, the mothers did now know their babies were dead. Some stories funny, some make you cry. There is a father who carried his child from Quang Tri, long way, and he carried baby in bag at his back. He left in a hurry, and something made his baby move out of the bag. Many rounds of mortar were coming overhead and a dog jumped into the bag, but the man didn't know. They all moved in the night time, and so when he stopped to let the child out of the bag, the dog jumped out. Sorry, no child, only a dog. The boy was fifteen months, and the man cried and cried and tried to die, but we saved him. I close for here with all my loves.

Diep

My letters seemed repetitious, filled with the same pleas, the same concerns:

Dearest Diep,

Your letter was received today. My worry is that if you wait much longer in Da Nang, there will be no way you will be permitted to leave. I contacted the Vietnamese Embassy here, and they told me you would need to apply for a passport and visa at the Ministry of the Interior in Saigon, and I've sent them the copy of the notarized affidavit promising that I'll be responsible for your support once you are here.

Can you get to Saigon? Is there some way that I could get money to you for the trip? Diep, I know how terribly hard it is for you to leave your family, and if you didn't have the children you might not consider it. But you might be doing your family more good by leaving there. If you were in a free country, you could earn money to send to them somehow. It is not impossible if you move quickly. The man at the embassy told me so. Please try not to be afraid. We will help you all we can when you get out of Vietnam. The fact that you have been working for the U.S. Army would be helpful to you *now,* but who knows how long that will last?

I am writing to the Secretary of Defense and have already contacted our Congressmen for advice and help. I'll write President Nixon himself, if I have to. Of course I mean for you to bring your children here with you. It would never occur to me for you to leave them behind. I hope that wasn't what was responsible for your delay in getting out of Da Nang?

Love,
Jann

Another letter went off to Waldie's offices:

Lynn Lacassie
Case Administrator
District Office
Congressman Jerome Waldie
805 Las Juntas Street
Martinez, CA 94553

Dear Ms. Lacassie:

Following our communication last summer, I contacted the Catholic Relief Services as you suggested. I was advised that Father C. was still in South America. They were unable to find out anything about Diep's health and situation. If there is anything that can be done, taking into consideration that (1) she worked loyally for our government for ten years as librarian for Army Special Services in Da Nang, (2) her children are Amerasian, (3) she was married to an American who has since returned without her to the United States, and (4) given all of the above, she is in great jeopardy if the Viet Cong gain power in Da Nang.

Between your offices and whatever the Catholic Relief Services are able to do, maybe she and her children can be saved. Please contact me as soon as possible. Time is running out, I am sure of it. With gratitude for anything you can do, I remain cordially yours,

                                                Jann Jansen

The reply was pleasant and courteous, explaining that before anyone could pursue the case further, I would need to get from Diep letters from her former superiors verifying that she had, indeed, been an employee for the library as she said. Frustrated, I wrote to her and informed her what was needed. Apparently the letter was not received, and one and a half months later, on January 20, 1975, I wrote her about it again.

Dearest Sister Diep,

Each time I write you, I wonder how many more letters of mine will arrive in your hands. I am also afraid that my letters will cause you trouble, more trouble than you now have. I am frantic to help you. Even if our letters are intercepted, always know that you will never be forgotten. If there is a way, we will find it. Please continue to write if you can and if it is wise. . . .

Love,
Jann

She wrote back on February 4, 1975.

Dear Sister Jannice,

For months now I not receive your letters. I fear you have forgotten me, as God has forgotten Vietnam. Perhaps you are very busy with your family and children. I understand. You are the fairy godmother to me and my children. You are the hope. I pray you not lose us. . . .

Diep

A week later I sent off papers that Diep needed to get out of Vietnam.

Dear Diep,

Here are copies of your important papers which you mailed me last year. I still have other copies here if you need them. The "Certificates of Good Character" are in a separate mailing.

Please leave Da Nang any way you can.

Jann

Her letter of March 24, 1975, which I did not receive until late April, brought frustrating news.

Dear Sister Jannice,

Many people die here today. War is all around. Babies, old people, the young boys . . . it is horrible. My heart is torn. Please, if I get out I will work for you, clean your house, do anything.

Please send papers.

Diep

Horrified, I wrote back at once, sending a second letter with copies of her papers. Again, she wrote to say she was waiting for her papers. Frantic, I wrote her back.

Dearest Diep,

Your second letter just arrived, and I am hoping that you have already received my letter and the originals of your papers, which I mailed to you last Saturday, nearly one week ago. I am sending you more copies in one other letter, so that if one doesn't get through, perhaps the other will.

Dearest Sister, you are too fine to be anyone's servant! You will be cared for, as will your children, by us. We are trying to do what we can. Larry has contacted the Vietnamese Consulate once again in San Francisco for information. Please do everything you can from that end. If you can, board a plane or boat, anything. We will gladly sponsor you or your children, but do not know how to go about that. We are trying. Have faith and do what you can, as we are. I pray that you will arrive safely here and be with us. MOVE IN HASTE. THERE IS NO TIME!

Love,
Jann

The date of that last letter was April 25, 1975.

"Lady," the woman behind the counter at the post office said gently, "haven't you been watching the news? The chances that your friend will get your letter are pretty slim at this point."

"Let's send it anyway," I said, fighting back tears.

"Okay, but it's a waste of your money. I doubt if it'll be delivered. Everything's coming back, you know."

"Please. I want to send it."

Two weeks later the letter to Diep appeared in my own mailbox with "Return to Sender, Service Suspended, Undeliverable" stamped all over it.

We had lost each other after all.

The sense of futility, of being lost in the true sense, overwhelmed me. In my mind, I was once again standing huddled against the hospital wall in Children's Hospital, holding onto myself as if I would surely fall apart otherwise, trying to grasp the meaning of my loss. Had all my hopes and prayers, all my feeble efforts ended with a letter that would never be delivered? I was tormented by the picture of one more innocent human being, suffering, perhaps being tortured or starved or even murdered with her children. Even worse, I wondered if I could have done more. Could I have prevented this single tragedy? In spite of everything, I had once again lost someone very dear.

Chapter Six

Survivors

Evacuees struggled toward the U.S. helicopters atop the Pittman apartments in Saigon. Human suffering was reduced to figures like "1.5 million Vietnamese killed, thousands fleeing their country," "57,931 Americans dead in Vietnam," "nearly 2,500 men and women (both civilians and servicemen) unaccounted for."

As Larry and I watched the drama unfold on television and in magazines and newspers, I tried to be detached, objective; I tried to accept the philosophy that every person has some purposeful destiny to fulfill and that I could not be a part of the lessons and experiences that Diep had to undergo. Whatever she had to go through, she had to go through, and it was not part of any divine plan that I would intervene. This had been Dottie's philosophy all along, and now I tried to accept it.

I tried to put out of my mind the chaos at Tan Son Nhut airport on that sad day of April 30, 1975, the stories of boat people drowning or suffering starvation in their attempts to reach freedom, the photographs of the Amerasian children—homeless, desperate pariahs.

"If she's alive, you'll hear from her one day," Larry said. "You've done all you can do." At times I believed that. It was when I questioned it that I felt the pain.

By the fall of 1975 I had still not heard from Diep. I had been hired that August to teach at Diablo Valley College on a part-time basis and was also giving piano lessons in my home and working as a traveling tutor for a large high-school district.

Although I continued to be plagued with migraines, I did not find them as severe or incapacitating as before. There was residual pain, of course, but I learned to live with it without a constant stream of painkillers. By 1975, I knew that I was truly recovering from the physical and emotional hurts of the previous decade. And I was putting unhealthy things behind me.

I was occasionally assigned to work with teenagers who had a drug dependency or severe emotional problems, and for a time I worked in a psychiatric hospital tutoring teenagers. From both these experiences, I discovered a strength within myself that emerged from my need to nurture and from the empathy that my own sorrows had produced. The adage that you cannot dwell on your own problems if you concentrate on someone else's proved true.

Although I thought about Diep, most of the time I tried to relegate my worries about her to the back of my mind. Then one day I received a letter from her sister Minh in Saigon, now Ho Chi Minh City.

It seemed that Minh continued to have better luck than Diep. She told me that Diep and her younger daughter had gone to the New Economic Zone, a primitive region that the Communist government had designated for agricultural development, as well as for penal detention. Diep was all right, she assured me, and would write to me when she had the opportunity.

Later, in a letter dated February of 1977, Diep described those first days and weeks that just preceded and immediately followed the fall of Saigon:

. . . I thought about how selfish I be with my girls. When I used to take them as babies to library where I worked, I was mean, too. I wanted them close to me, but if we were killed, we would all be killed together. I wanted to be a good mother and have them be proud of me. But at 29 I was the same as young widow. I could not marry anyone now in Vietnam, and I didn't want to see my children hurt. Many children of the American father and Vietnamese mother lived in the streets, their mothers afraid of the Communists who would punish them for having the American child. I did not want my children to suffer. And then I found the affection and kindness coming from you, and was surprised and blessed. I knew that God had blessed me for something and had not forgotten me when you tried to give us comfort and encourage us.

After 1973 I had known the war would stop and the Americans would go home, and we would lose. The SVN government very weak at that time. The Vietnamese did not want the Vietnamese and American blood all over the country. I thought that Americans would be sorry to watch us die. When our President Thieu said: "Don't believe what the Viet Cong say, just watch what they do," he was right. Now most of Vietnam remembers these words. They were true.

The worst times were then in Spring of 1975, the bad days. Da Nang was full of death in war. Many refugees were there, believing Da Nang would still belong to the

South Vietnam government. I remember the faces of the soldiers in that war, the young boys so young and innocent, and took pity.

My poor young brother and his friends . . . they frightened when they saw the death all around and had been called to fight. Everywhere we went there were dead bodies in the streets. The blood was on the streets, and people could die for anything and for nothing. We were so confused. By the riverside near my home, many people die. Some soldiers so crazy now they found it easy to kill, and they believed they would be killed at any time, and so they had fun in killing anything that moved the wrong way.

I think now about my friends I will never see again. I think about the young widows in both our countries. I recall my friend Thi. She and her husband had been married five years with two small children. I remember the day in New Year Tet when she and her husband drove the jeep from Quang Ngai to Da Nang, seventy miles, and on the way her husband was killed. She wept, driving her dead husband and two little children to Da Nang.

Diep described in later conversations with me how one of her young stepbrothers, already depressed and anguished by the suffering all around him, became devastated when his best friend committed suicide.

"His good friend had taken a bottle of malaria pills and had died quickly," she told me. "Hieu, my stepbrother, wrote me a letter that said: 'Dearest Sister Diep, everyone in this life has to die anyway. I do not want to live. Do not be sad when I am dead. I just wish everyone good luck. Jeanie and Jolie, try to study well and eat your soup. Don't cry. That is the best way to live.' He took thirty malaria pills just like his friend, and died fifteen minutes before I receive the letter, they told me.''

Some family members were choosing suicide rather than face the continued poverty, hunger, and threatened Communist reprisals. The new government observed these incidents and gave the order that if anyone in a family committed suicide, the surviving family members would be heavily fined. The precarious monetary system was such that Vietnamese who might have taken their own lives now had another consideration: the possibility of leaving their loved ones entirely destitute.

Diep wrote about the fate of the baby she had adopted. He was fifteen months old when his mother, pregnant with another baby and poor, came to Diep and asked her to take the child. For some time Diep had made him a part of her little family, feeding and clothing the youngster, until one morning the baby's mother came back for him. She believed that the boy's father was returning and that he would take them out of Vietnam. It did not happen, however.

. . . Well, she was very poor, no food for herself or her baby, and she was not too smart, either. The baby boy got sick. She had no money for medicine and came to me, and I gave her some money. But the baby got worse, and she could not afford medicine, so she tried to bleed him—the Chinese way—to get the poisons out. He died, and she could not bury him.

I say, ''Bring the baby to me. I'll give the man some money who bury him.'' So very sad! She gave the baby body to me, and we buried him in little box.

Then my brother—18 or 19 then—and his friends came to my house in Da Nang. They had run off from their soldier unit, deserters, they say, and I told them they would cause me much trouble, but I hide them for two days. They were so young, so frightened: "We lose. We lose our country," they say. I finally made them go back.

Later, she described to me her grief at having to send her young brother back into the hell he had tried to escape, an act that haunted her.

"Together my aged father, stepmother and little sisters planned to leave Da Nang. I remember the long looks I saved for my house, knowing that if I ever returned, it might belong to strangers, Communists, and all my things as well. A sweet lady who had liked me at the evening language school said she would take my daughters to my sister's house in Saigon. I was so relieved to have them go, and once again wondered if we would meet again. The air was filled with rockets, dangerous every minute now. My daughters then went ahead with the American lady, and I was to follow.

"Together my sisters, father and stepmother and I went down Da Nang River in small boat to the Da Nang harbor. People crying, babies crying for their lost mothers. I just shut my eyes. What could I do? We were in a small boat, not very sturdy, and so close to the shore that we could see all of the pain and tears.

"In Da Nang harbor we tried to climb aboard the big American ship, I think it was *USS Miller?* It was so easy to fall back into the water. I was so scared. Then I couldn't forget! Thirty hours no food, no water in my stomach. Some mothers killed their babies by accident by giving them saltwater, they were so thirsty! I was so hungry and thirsty, and I couldn't say much. I could not walk well. I thought in my mind: 'If I could eat something first, then

I could die.' I had accepted it now. Then we arrived at the beach after the American boat had landed us at Cam Ranh Bay. I saw escape now, but had little money left after paying for the ship.''

Diep told me about how people brought everything they could carry to the large ships: motorcycles, television sets, anything that meant something to them.

"People, they climbed and pushed. Hurry, hurry, V.C. behind us coming down from Central Highlands. I had felt so little, so frail when climbing down those sandbag walls to get off the ship. People said: 'Come! Hurry, hurry!' when they see me get off. 'The ship over there goes to the Philippines,' someone said, but I just shake my head.

" 'My children are in Saigon, and it is Saigon where I go.'

"Someone said, 'You are crazy. Save yourself.'

" 'It doesn't matter if I save my life if I don't have my children,' I told them.

" 'We are lucky the *USS Miller* ship set safely in Cam Ranh Bay,' someone said. 'Now, here is your opportunity to find the safe and free life.'

"I shut my eyes. I shut my eyes to all I leave behind, and to the safety there ahead, and shut my eyes to my innocent young girlhood gone with my lost loves. I now opened my eyes for the life and love of my sweet children. The *USS Miller* was covered with clothes and forsaken bundles of things we Vietnamese could not take with us, no way to carry on foot, and with the things left behind on the ship I left my chance once again to escape. I watched the ship pull away without me, many Vietnamese on board going to the Philippines and safety.

"Now I travel alone to find my children in Saigon.''

* * *

A thick fog had set in along the waters, making the air damp and cold. Diep heard screaming not far away and saw a familiar sight. "Many people die in seconds because too many tried to climb into small boats." Many people were in a panic, knowing that the Viet Cong were hours or at the most just days away.

In the growing darkness, refugees moved silently, stoically, along the road. Many were soldiers, like Diep's young brother, who had realized they were beaten and who joined the throngs of people fleeing with all their possessions on their backs.

She did not know how she would make that journey to Saigon. Not only did she face nearly two hundred miles on foot, but she would have to face all kinds of peril on the way. Crazed from starvation or thirst, people might seize her and rob her if they guessed that she had any money at all. Few vehicles passed along the road out of Cam Rahn now, and when they did they drove as quickly as they could to prevent refugees from attempting to climb aboard.

One jeep carrying several ARVN soldiers ran down an old couple in the road when the two could not get out of the way, and they lay dying on the road, another truck passed over them only a few feet from where Diep was walking. She heard the sound of breaking bones and their dying moans.

The world had gone mad, turned upside down in a frenzy of killing. Along the wharf Diep saw bodies stacked like the day's catch of fish: impersonal, distorted, in raglike piles. She moved faster along the road amid the silently moving caravan of refugees.

History records many such desperate wartime marches

of the homeless and hungry, forced to flee invaders. Every war has a common image of innocents who must leave behind everything they have toiled for, everything of value, sometimes the very necessities they have struggled their entire lifetimes to acquire.

Diep recalled her letters to me, in which she had predicted that she would be in this situation. Once, they were mere words in a letter, and now her prophesies—prophesies she had never really believed would come true—were fulfilled. She was indeed a refugee of war.

When she stopped to get a drink at a stream of muddy water near the road, the face that looked back at her from the murky water was that of a tired and sorrowful woman. The blank expression and the vacant eyes were like those of all the other refugees she had traveled with that day. She again took her place among the homeless who moved onward to whatever fate lay in store for them. Always in the back of her mind was the picture of two sweet-faced children, arms outstretched, calling to their mother, a picture that made her quicken her pace.

It was a full day's steady walk from Cam Ranh to Phan Rang. There were about seven sites in the province of Phan Rang that received refugees, and Diep—exhausted and dusty from her long journey—sought refuge in one of them, an abandoned bus station. She found water but was told that there was no food. "You'll have to go on to Ham Tan if you want food," she was informed. That would have been at least several hours more on foot in the darkness. She chose to sleep, hungry, in the station.

Around 3:00 A.M. Diep awoke, hearing a baby cry, and she saw a tearful mother trying to nurse her wailing child. She worried about the baby and then thought about her own little girls. The stories that circulated among the weary refugees about Saigon's impending fall frightened her, and she rose and fled into the night at a run.

"I would find a shelter," she told me, "and food in Ham Tan, and then be stronger for the journey to Saigon and my children. That night I passed many sorry people, some sick, others wanting to die by the road, saying they go no farther. One man begged his wife to kill him, and she wept and tried but could not. She only injure him more, then had to leave him there. In the dark I felt safe, but frightened, my heart pounding so hard inside my chest that I could hardly breathe, my side aching so bad that I could barely walk at times. The sky would suddenly light up with rockets, and I heard them strike nearby. The fighting was all around."

A little after dawn she arrived at a beautiful spot on a sandy beach about eight miles south of Phan Rang. The South China Sea stretched serenely as far as she could see, and she wondered how many refugees from different wars had looked on this quiet and beautiful spot. She told me that she had wished then that she could instantly be transformed into one of the peaceful birds in the marsh before her.

"I wanted the peace from war, the chance to sleep until it passed. I wanted to lie down among the marshes and be as tranquil as the little frog, with no care for tomorrow. But Saigon was going to die, and there was no time. I did not know how I would get there. The distance just from Cam Ranh to the small city of Ham Tan in Binh Tuy Province was one hundred and fifty miles! It would be another eighty miles at least traveling to Saigon itself. I could not become accustomed to seeing the bodies, but after awhile the smell was not noticed. It was as common as the salt air from the sea.

"I rested awhile on the beach in a cove, and then saw a truck pull over on the road above. I ran to the driver and asked for a ride to Ham Tan. "We take you only to Phan Thiet," he said, *"if* you have money." I had a little, and gave it. Then I saw the people crowded among debris and bundles in the back of the truck, like cargo or sheep to slaughter.

"The truck very bouncy, but we not mind. I closed my eyes and ears to poor people trying to climb in the truck and being pushed off. People begging for ride. I was afraid."

Diep tried to sleep but could not. Huddled with silent refugees on that trip to Phan Thiet, she witnessed war in all its grisly, crimson horror. "For three years I would not be able to touch the red meat of beef," she told me later. "For three years, when I looked at the red beef and yellow fat, I would see the human dead bodies. They just the same!" Her eyes would widen in awe at the recollection.

Life, death, life, death. One moved on, unable to fear what was beyond control, beyond one's ability to protect or save. Her face was now the face of every homeless, horror-stricken, sick refugee. As she moved in the direction of her children, they were the sole force that propelled her. She visualized her children in her sister's house, beckoning to her. They needed her. Amid the shouting insanity of war, the silence of despair, the stench of death, they were all that kept her pushing forward into the night and the growing darkness.

Desperate people who move away from death, yet are forced to accept it and are dulled by it, are often silent. Diep's visions of hell had stunned her, anesthetized her into numbness. Her girls were in Saigon; her maternal instincts and devotion gave her the strength to endure whatever her God demanded to reach them.

She recalled: "I saw Vietnamese writing on wall as we passed. Over and over it say: VIETNAM, WE GRIEVE FOR YOU TODAY. VIETNAM, WE GRIEVE FOR YOU. I weep for my country, my beautiful country, for all the generations who had known only war here, and for the generations who would not be. Why, God, I asked as the truck took me to Phan Thiet, must this small country be so important to the Communists? Why would men like to kill the little children and old ones? I felt ashamed that God did not answer in such a time as this, and that I doubted He was really there.

"I had left Da Nang on March 26th. The Communists right behind me. They entered Da Nang on Sunday, March 30th.

And within four days, the military forces defending the four major cities along South Vietnam's coast had fled, just as Diep's brother had done, heading south toward Saigon.

ARVN troops—demoralized, drunken, crazed—rampaged through the cities, destroying everything in their way. They looted, they frequently shot at randomly moving targets, no matter who or what, and they slaughtered fleeing civilians who tried to board boats or other vehicles. They even shot at each other. They seemed driven to crush underfoot any semblance of sanity. It had happened so quickly, this change from a rumbling distant threat to the chaos Diep now witnessed. She left the truck and stumbled along the road in a daze.

"We are refugees of man's madness," she thought to herself.

The walk to Ham Tan was long and tiring after the arduous truck ride, and once again she hid among the marshes and slept. By noon she was walking again, then was fortunate enough to board a rickety bus headed for Saigon that had pulled over to let off a dying old man.

She recalled the scene when she arrived in Saigon: "My children so happy to see me, they thought I was dead. I rested at my sister Minh's house, glad to be alive, trying to put the horrible sights of the road out of my mind, trying to forget the suffering people out of my memory too. My sister, she afraid of the fall of Saigon, and we decided we would go to the embassy if we could sell Minh's house and things first. Perhaps we could get plane to Thailand or the United States.

Twenty-one-year-old Jeanie later gave a tape-recorded account of that time:

"The war, the report of a gun, the death all around, were images of my childhood. They are images which will be in my mind forever. The sobs and screams of women who cried for their husbands will forever be in my ears.

"I remember before being taken to Saigon to my aunt's home, just before the end of that city, a winter night in Da Nang. When I had fallen asleep, suddenly I heard a loud sound, the noise of a gun, cannon, anti-aircraft, planes. I don't know how to express my fear of that time. I closed my eyes but could not sleep again. My mother took everybody in my family to kneel in front of our altar. She prayed for peace and safety for us as the guns were heard not far away. From that night on—I was a little girl of nine—I knew to be afraid. War and death: I've known those words many times since then.

"The following morning I learned that the fighting had been with the Viet Cong and Vietnamese Army outside of Da Nang, and one of the dead was my neighbor. My girl friend and I went to the dead man's home. He was a soldier, and his young wife was pregnant for three months. Her name was Suong, about thirty-five years old. Her dead husband was captain of the infantry army. They had four sons, and the oldest was a classmate of mine.

"When I came there, I saw crowds of people who were relatives, friends of the dead man. I didn't see Mrs. Suong, the poor woman in pain. I only saw my classmate. He was crying and sitting in front of his dead father's bed. Then he and his brother cried: 'Why did you leave us alone in this great darkness, Daddy?' They wept and repeated this sorrowful question over and over.

"I have seen the faces of so many who have borne such suffering, and I know the faces well. I would always ask myself: Why did the war always happen in this poor country? But I was so young that I could not answer that question!

"I went home nearby to prepare my books for my studies in school and have my lunch, but I could not eat anymore. Images of the dead man with blood still on his face, the sobs of my classmate and his mother's friends, the smell of smoke, incense, and blood mixed made me sad and dizzy.

"In school my mind was taken away until my teacher came into the class and everybody stood up to greet him. I saw my face in a glass near my desk and thought I looked like an adult, although I was only nine years old. But a young girl leaves the body quickly during wartime, and the woman must come in.

"April 30, 1975, was the death day of Saigon, the day that Vietnamese will never forget. In the early morning of that day, everything seemed strange and quiet, as if waiting. We had not slept the night before. I was still in bed and heard the sound of a car outside my house. Suddenly, my mother and aunt came in and urged me, Jolie, and Freddy, my cousin, to prepare our clothes for our escape."

One of Diep's letters described that day:

. . . We had tried to sell the house, sell anything for three weeks.

But no one wanted the house besides the soldiers who fled from the war. Now I saw that we would have no money for passage out of here if the house could not be sold. We tried and tried, but people only wanted rice and clothes. Some went from house to house, as in Da Nang before, begging for a little rice to feed their starving families.

Minh and I waited too late once again, not knowing what to do. Without any money, it was no use going to American Embassy, but we took what we had and left for the embassy on April 30th. We were there that terrible time. . . .

Diep, her sister, nephew, and two little girls were in that panicky throng depicted in a now-famous photograph taken at the U.S. Embassy on the afternoon of April 30 when Vietnamese had to be beaten off the barbed-wire fence atop a wall. Masses of frightened Vietnamese surrounded the embassy, all with stories of loyalty and promises that had been made to them. Would the Americans really abandon them to the V.C.? Would the kind U.S. president really give up on them? They tried to force their way through to be in line for the helicopters that whisked American dependents and select Vietnamese off into the safety of the skies.

Diep vividly recalled the scene years later:

"We were there trying to push our children ahead of the crowds of people. Late that afternoon, helicopters come, taking people from the roof, people dashing to be first. Many people hurt. My daughters, they little and I was afraid they be trampled in the mobs. We waited all day, trying to get aboard, but we could not. People begged, pushed and begged, and there was no way.

"I thought we had seen people crazy before, but now it was different. No one hurried away with the things they stole. They took their time going through things in the embassy, taking pictures and things that were personal to people only hours before.

"Money on floor and no one care. People taking anything they could carry away, even silly things. I thought: If they so crazy, perhaps they want to show the Viet Cong they don't like Americans. I don't know. Some Vietnamese soldiers got very drunk. They started little fires in the embassy and around. One American he tell me that there would be more the next day come to take the rest of us. Someone had big laugh and ask what he was drinking. 'This is the end of a culture,' someone said. 'This is the last day of the South Vietnamese life.'

"I knew that everything would be changed. I knew that I had missed my decisions over and over, so now I would pay the price. I had so many regrets.

"When I saw some Americans upstairs who did not go, I tried to go up the stairs and push the girls ahead of me. There were two helicopters trying very hard to land, and so many people rushed forward to be in [one] that they could not go. People fell backward, some very hurt. Helicopters were afraid then to land. Tear gasses were thrown at us to keep us away, and grenades I think were thrown to disband the many people. I think the American Marines were afraid of the panicky people.

"The tear gasses made me not see. My children could not see and cried. We run inside and got water to wash our faces, and I saw the kind American soldiers in the helicopters and said: 'Please save my children. They have same skin color and hair color as you.'

" 'If he lands, he won't be able to fly off,' someone said. Too many people. We had lost our decision once again.

"I heard the president announce the welcome of the North Vietnam government, and I went home with tears. We lost Saigon. We lost everything. On the way home, it was rainy, and when I came in the door my daughters say that God cried for Vietnam that day.

"On the streets people had risen in revolt, but now it was quiet. Where did they go? There were dead bodies in different places around. I didn't want to see. I was very sorry for the poor Vietnamese soldiers with no place to go, no place to hide in their uniform. Some Vietnamese gave the soldiers clothes to change. Many died in their uniform. The Communist soldiers came to town with indifferent cold faces, so quiet, so cold. They made me afraid of the days to come."

Diep's daughter Jeanie added her recollections of that day:

"When we got to the embassy that afternoon, many people were there with their pitiful belongings like tables, chairs, telephones, many things. From one of the rooms in the embassy we watched and thought, 'We don't need

to take anything. All we want is to leave Saigon in time.'
Everywhere we looked, we saw papers from file cabinets
all over the floors, drawers pulled out of the file cabinets on the floor, money—people fighting over things they
took from the consulate's offices.

"I was nine years old, but I was afraid to go back home
when we could not get upstairs and be taken off by the
helicopter. Below on the street we walked around many
dead bodies, and shirts from many soldiers who had fled
the war. Weapons of all kinds were thrown down in the
roads. But somewhere we heard the report of a gun from
soldiers who wanted to be hero soldiers and fight until the
end, although their army was disintegrated. That was a
sad memory.

"My mother told us that most of the former soldiers
had gone to the re-education camp in North Vietnam or
Central Highlands. No one knew if they would ever come
back."

And so the girls, Freddy, and the two distraught women,
their eyes reddened from the tear gas and crying, returned
home. Their last memories of the Americans would be the
sight of nearly a dozen Marines on the roof of the building
unloading canister after canister of tear-gas grenades on
the heads of the Vietnamese crowded around the edges of
the building below them. "We understood why they did
it," Diep said philosophically.

"It seemed no one lived there anymore," Jeanie said,
describing Saigon after its capture. "All was quiet in waiting. Cars were left at the roadside by people who would
never want them again. Many people still waited, I heard,
on top of the roof, hoping helicopters would come back
for them. Some were Vietnamese, but some were Americans, too.

"Everything was tense. There was no happiness to greet the Viet Cong when they come into city. They looked so young, just boys maybe a few years older than me, sometimes. Everything was quiet in respect for the death of our country."

Once back at Minh's house, the family remained silent and sad. No one could speak. The children—old beyond their years and realizing their mother's fear—did not play or talk among themselves.

Diep recalled that day:

"At the end of the day when we went home all sad and forlorn, we said nothing. We knew all was lost, that the V.C. were on the way and would soon be in Saigon. The smoke from their burning could already be seen in the sky. There was only one thing to do. I had found some leaves from a poison tree in the forest and had kept them just in case. Minh went to the pharmacy and bought some pills for sleeping. We decided that we would first kill the children and then ourselves. It was not uncommon. Many people afraid of the V.C. did this, choosing the peacefulness of the death to the suffering of the life.

"We could not leave our children, and we did not want to live with the Communist government. Minh and I had seen the way the half-American children lived. We with the half-breed American babies knew they had no future now in Vietnam. They would be treated very bad, worse than the dog, no opportunity, no education, made fun of and badly abused.

"Minh tried to poison their rice, but we cried together so much and somehow the children knew why. They wouldn't eat. They were afraid of us. They were angry and afraid and did not trust us for a long time. Minh and I didn't know what to do, we were so confused. No one would protect us, we with the American children."

Jeanie, Jolie, and Freddy told their mothers that if they killed them, the children would ask God to punish their mothers severely. Diep and Minh didn't know what to do. They were aware of those neighbors who had panicked and entered into family suicide pacts when it was learned that the Viet Cong were about to invade Saigon. Diep and Minh tried on more than one occasion to carry out their plan, but each time they were so overcome by grief at the prospect of murdering their children that they resigned themselves to whatever their fate would be with the Communist takeover.

Minh's son, seven-year-old Freddy, told her, "I won't call you 'Mother' anymore, but will call you 'Miss Minh.' You are not my mother if you can kill me." The three children even went on a hunger strike, actually afraid to eat anything their mothers prepared for them.

The sad part of this is that for a long time the children did not trust Diep or Minh. They refused to eat unless they were certain that the food was not poisoned, and Diep would long recall her children pleading on that fateful evening in April of 1975 to let them live.

"Please, Mama," they told her, "we won't eat much, and we will be good and mind . . ."

In two weeks' time, Diep's anxiety over having left her home in Da Nang became almost unbearable. Things seemed to be settling down in Saigon, and after talking with people who knew members of the Communist police, she decided that it would now be safe to return home. After all, she reasoned, the war was over, and the fighting had stopped. There might be peace at last.

Her immediate fears assuaged, Diep and her daughters started off toward Da Nang, at least a week's journey.

While Jeanie, Jolie, and Diep were waiting for the bus

that would take them to Phan Thiet, a Viet Cong soldier spotted them. "Aha," he called to his friends, "there is an American girl out of her country."

"*Not* American," little Jolie cried out. "*Russian!*"

"You American," the young Communist soldier taunted her. "Your hair is brown, and you are not Vietnamese."

"I am Vietnamese, and I am Russian, too!" the child shot back. Her courage and defiance for one so tiny amused the men, and they shrugged her off.

Diep was to tell me during one of our conversations later:

"It was then I knew for sure that my daughters would not be able to admit their blood was half-American for a long, long time. It was that day that I looked at my two sweet little girls and knew I would have many troubles trying to protect them. American or Russian, it was not good for Vietnamese to be mixed, and the men—they would not respect my virtuous daughters."

The road they traveled with stoic and silent fellow passengers was littered with the debris and grisly horrors of the Viet Cong's passage. Villages had been burned; starving dogs, their ribs protruding and their eyes bulging from hunger and misery, wandered around, looking for anything they could scavenge. Quite often, they resorted to the bodies of the fallen villagers, and when Diep saw this she closed her mind to it. "This is the way things must be," she told herself. "I cannot change it."

An old man—perhaps sixty-five—sat near them on the bus. He was fascinated with Jeanie, with her large brown eyes and fragile body. After hours of travel, during which he thoughtfully appraised the child, he politely asked Diep some questions about Jeanie. Diep shook her head and hardly acknowledged him, but he persisted.

As he spoke about his good fortune in not losing everything because of the war, how sensible and wise he had been in preparing for the "Liberation Day," Diep felt chilled. She knew what was coming.

"I will give you much money for that child," he said as he gestured toward Jeanie. Diep told him No emphatically.

The man was quiet for a long time. Then he started up the one-sided conversation once again. He described his home outside of Cam Rhan and his young daughter who needed someone since his wife had gone away. "I would pay you well for your other daughter," he said. "She looks very American and will only be the cause of much trouble for you. Besides, you will probably have to go to the re-education camp in Ban Me Thuot, and it is unlikely that your daughters can go along. They are so young."

Again, Diep felt a chill. Her heart pounded, and the fear must have shown in her eyes. The children were worried for the their mother, not comprehending the man's intentions at all.

"The girls stay with me, no matter what," Diep said dismissing him.

The journey to Da Nang took them eight days. As they walked down their street, Diep saw her house in the distance and knew at once what lay ahead. Three men were sitting near the open doorway drinking something. They seem nonchalant as she approached.

"This is my house," she said angrily.

"No more," one of the men told her. "We can give you something, but this house is too big for your small family. It is needed. No one must have more than he needs."

* * *

Within a fortnight, Diep was visited by the Communist police assigned to her area. She was told that she would have to report to the Central Highlands; she could take the children with her, but they would be forced to work alongside her if she did. First, they said, she would be sent to a re-education camp for one hundred days of education and deprogramming. The attitude of the policemen was so benign, she later recalled, that the insidious message they delivered seemed dreamlike and unreal.

Stories about what happened to those who had consorted with the Americans filled her with terror once again. She knew that there was no choice—she would have to do as she was told.

"I was a refugee, a helpless woman. What could I do? I made plans to take my children with me to the camp; we would learn about the new government together." Deep within, however, Diep knew that she would never buckle down to the Communists; she would be alive and free *inside* herself, and she vowed to outwit them every chance she had. She would pretend to play their games, but in reality she would cheat them whenever she could.

The papers for her passage to the re-education camp were issued, and she was relieved to hear rumors that it was not as brutal a place as another camp farther north. She would not be mistreated as badly there as at the camp where she learned her brother had been taken.

Chapter Seven

A New Life with No Hope

I received a letter addressed to me in Minh's neat handwriting, and before I could open it, I felt despair descend like a shadow that covered everything around me. The fact that it was not Diep's handwriting on the envelope made me start to cry in anticipation. In the letter, dated February 12, 1980, a saddened and ill Diep, exhausted after nearly five years of hard labor in the rice paddies and sugar fields, sent me a sad message.

Dearest Jannice,

It may be a long time before we ever speak to each other by way of letters again. I have asked my sister Minh to send this to you, but she may have trouble doing it.

I want you to know if I die here that your love and kindness has been the warm fire that keep away the chill. You have been my sweet sister with no reason but love and kindness to watch out for me. Many times I had the chance to leave this place, but my love for my country and my not belief that it would die kept me here. I had such confusion all the time. Some said we would be saved by the Americans, that we would not be left. Some said that Vietnam's history for 150 years has been war and occupation, that it was our fate.

Well, I spent my whole life learning the ways of a cultured lady, refined, knowing only the books and wanting the education for me and my girls. I never placed my hands in the soil. Now, I am to work with the soil and bend my back to the ground. This is my new life. I have no choice. This will be my entire life now, until I can work no more. . . .

Diep also said that in preparation for her journey by bus to the Ban Me Thuot camp, she had felt compelled to burn all of my letters. If the Communist authorities found such things among her possessions, it would be hard for her. She destroyed anything that connected her with the Americans, with the exception of a tattered and underexposed photograph of Jolie's father. This she hid carefully among her meager possessions. All around her people solemnly carted their only belongings in rolls and boxes on their backs, moving silently in orderly fashion as the guards directed them to the bus.

She would never forget that hot, muggy day when she and her small children got off the crowded, rickety bus. The ground was dry and parched as far as she could see. Very little land had been cleared by the families already living there. "This is your land parcel," Diep and her children were told, as about 1,000 square meters of land were pointed out to them, land that had been cordoned off and would soon be oozing red clay when the monsoons arrived.

Diep was shown the newly created rice paddies and told that she would have to help dig new irrigation systems. The guards hovered around them all the time, she discovered. The guards were called *Du Kich* and were often recruited from the new arrivals. Sometimes they were "crazy people" who turned on the others and were totally unpredictable. The policemen *(Cong An)* were feared for another reason. "If they took you, no one ever heard from you again. You just disappeared. In jail? Maybe, but you were gone from the earth as far as your family and friends knew," Diep later told me.

Since rice is the staple food for the Vietnamese, the rice crops are of critical importance. The annual allowance Diep was promised when she first arrived was 200 kilos. The amount never increased and, in fact, decreased each year. "It became harder, not easier, to find enough food," she said.

"You'll have a year's supply of food," she was told when she first arrived at Ban Me Thuot, "but when that runs out, you had better have your crops ready for harvesting. There will be no more allotments." Of course, the amount of allocated food was not enough for that first year, but this was a way of guaranteeing that their workers' agricultural labors would be of primary importance.

Before the fall of Saigon in 1975, the normal Vietnamese diet, besides rice, included pork, fish, various soups laden with noodles, meats like tongue, heart, stomach, and a variety of intestines, coagulated animal blood, spices, hot peppers, a pungent fish sauce called *nuoc-mam,* soybean sauces, vegetables, fresh fruits, and, of course, green tea. One of the most popular foods was a soup called *pho,* which was sold everywhere on the streets.

Pho was the favorite Vietnamese snack, eaten for any meal at any time.

Now Diep and her children ate mostly rice and beans. As this was doled out so sparingly, she sought ways of "supplementing" it. The sympathetic Montagnards, or mountain people, cooperated with the Vietnamese by loaning them land in the forests on which to grow their own little gardens. This secret, kept from the Communist guards, meant that Diep and her children often had to walk for miles at odd hours in order to tend their private garden surreptitiously. The success of the crops was literally a matter of life or death. If the crops were poor or failed, it meant death for the farmers.

"When the women complained about female problems, they were sometimes allowed to work in the homes preparing food for the others," Diep said. "They served the officials who were overseeing the labor. The guards stood with guns to make sure that people did not try to escape and go home, and to make sure everyone did his work."

They had "re-education meetings" which took place both at night and during the afternoons. Since work had to be accomplished during the daytime, it was not uncommon to attend meetings at night after ten to sixteen hours of labor. The leaders (as they were called) were both men and women. Diep felt a mixture of disgust and awe for the women guards: "We sometimes felt greater fear of them than the men," she said. "They were chosen because they were *big* women. They wore uniforms. They were mean, even kicking the men! We all sat around on the floors in the meeting building and the security guards made sure no one talked. Everyone listened carefully." The guards always wore guns.

She was to have one hundred days of "re-education." Prior to this, she spent three months working in the fields "so they could see how we adjusted." But once her ability to function under guard was established, she was required to attend the meetings several times a week at least, and often every day. "Confessions" were not spoken but were written down. Any infraction or alleged sign of disrespect was immediately dealt with, and it was inadvisable to admit that you knew how to speak English or had any sympathy with the Americans. Of course, Jolie and Jeanie were obvious indications to her captors that Diep had "known the enemy, and known him quite well."

Diep and her children built their own thatch-roof house in the Central Highlands with the help of "old men who knew about carpentry." The furnishings were crudely hewn beds and a chair and altar. At night they would sit huddled together, eating their soup or rice. An occasional snake would hang from the thatched roof or drop down to the floor. With more than sixty species of snakes in Vietnam and at least twenty of those poisonous, among them cobras, kraits, vipers, and a variety of deadly water snakes, the smart person dispatches the snake first and tries to identify it afterward.

Keeping rice, beans, and corn dry and free of vermin was an endless battle, and competing with rodents for the stored food was a serious challenge as well. If the rats won the competition, it could mean actual starvation for the humans, who were totally dependent on the food they stored.

Since mosquitoes bred prolifically in the canals where Diep and the girls worked, they worried constantly that they might come down with diseases transmitted by the insects, such as malaria or any of the other serious fevers that were striking down many of the people they knew. "Many get sick and die there," Diep said sadly. "We get eye infections too, and there is no medicine at all."

Not long after Diep had arrived in the Central Highlands New Economic Zone, she figured out the advantages of becoming a bookkeeper, the person who allocated rations to the other families. Due to her education and ability with numbers, she was assigned the job. This did not release her from working the crops, however. It was an added job, not a substitution for her regular manual labor.

At first there were eleven families for whom she had to keep records. She allowed them to keep more rice than the Communist leaders would have permitted, and she assisted them in every way she could—even when she imperiled herself in doing so. Her true feelings she kept to herself, feigning loyalty behind a false smile.

"I had spent my entire life working with my mind," she said. "Now the rest of my life would be spent working with my hands and my back. But I kept the workings of my mind silent from the Communist leaders. When they said we had one hundred days to learn re-education and the ways of how to live, I sweetly smile big smile and nod and say nothing."

That so-called Asian passivity which is really a form of self-control, is probably what saved her. She need only look at her daughters, old far beyond their years, to know that she would do whatever it took to survive—for them.

One of the few possessions she had taken with her to the Central Highlands was a pair of knitting needles. With these she began to make sweaters for the Communist leaders and working families as well. Her ingenuity paid off.

"I make sweaters out of old ones, using money some people have for yarn, too, and make sweaters for former soldiers, policemen, other people like me, and receive a little money to help us more." Her little capitalist "business" was conducted under the noses and with the blessing of the anti-capitalist regime. The humor was that no one in power ever saw the irony of it. Her sweaters were much admired and sought after. She could make a long-sleeved sweater for an adult in just a few days, often knitting by firelight late at night after putting in a long day at hard labor in the rice paddies.

About five miles from where Diep lived there was a bus stop with an office maintained by the police, and nearby were markets where bartering was common. It was here that Diep sometimes sold her sweaters.

To go to the city of Saigon, now called Ho-Chi-Minh City, was a three-day bus trip that cost the equivalent of one month's salary for a teacher. Should Diep receive permission to go, and should she be able to scrape up funds for the ticket, she then had the worry that someone would steal her money.

Even in their second year at the camp, Diep and her children had nearly starved, but by her fifth year there, she managed to win some recognition as a faithful re-educated lady and she was made "agricultural leader," a slight improvement over her position when she first arrived.

Gone was the graceful *ao-dai,* the beautiful overdress with form-fitting waist, tight sleeves, and panels that extended from the waist, front, and back, to cover long satin trousers. Now her uniform was a dark pajama-like outfit with a loose, shapeless jacket. Gone was the long black hair and in it place a bobbed, chopped, squared hairstyle that demanded no care.

It was considered a blatant symbol of American influence to wear nail polish. One woman who had not removed her nail polish had her fingers chopped off. "Now you work harder without fingers," Diep said the Communist leaders told the woman.

The climate, the insects, the outbursts of temper and threats by guards, the frequent illnesses that plagued them, all contributed to Diep's ordeal. Add to this her fragility—never before in her life had she toiled in this manner, having been brought up in a comfortable home. Compounding all this was her sense of desperation. As she told me several years later:

"When we came there, we were shown the former South Vietnamese soldiers digging the irrigation ditches in the forest. Their punishment was cruel and many died there. No food. No safe drink. They just work and work until they die. 'No problem to replace,' the Communist leaders say. There was no way to escape, no way to lie. The leaders would give each family member a form to fill out, and on it they would ask the same questions about everyone else. On my form it would say: 'Tell about Mr. Tran. What work did he do before the liberation? Does his family still own any property? What does he own now at this place?' And the questions would be asked of everyone about everyone else, so that if one of us did not tell the truth or forgot something, we could be severely punished. We did not know who told what. No one wanted to cause anyone else trouble. So I would answer questions about Mr. Tran the best I could.

"Then they ask same question of Mr. Nguyen. Then they ask same question of Mr. Le, and Mr. Tay Son, and Mr. Dinh! No one lie, because each form had to match up. Then Mr. Tran would be asked questions about each of the others, and so forth. All forms would be compared, and if one was different, he could be punished.

"We had no house when we first got there but stayed for a few months with another family. Our house was built with thatched roof and had dirt floor, beaten-down earth.

"I could not adjust to snakes at night, when they sometimes swung down from the thatched roof and hung before

us. There are oh, so very many snakes which are deadly
and kill you right away. Lots of rats and mice, and *leeches!*
We had to burn them off when we work in the rice fields.
Sometimes my daughters would hear me scream when the
yellow and black leeches found my feet, and they come to
my rescue with sharp machetelike blade. They not poison
you, but you bleed and bleed when they hang on, and
sometimes infection would come in the sores they make.''

In telling the story, Jolie and Jeanie would giggle and
recall how terrified their mother was of snakes and leeches.
Jeanie, an independent tomboy by Vietnamese standards,
seemed gleeful in her method of dispatching these
pests. She told how she had witnessed the leeches swim-
ming rapidly toward them as they worked barefoot in the
rice paddies, and how she sliced the creatures in half,
hacking away at them before they could attach themselves.

Lice was another problem, infesting people almost immediately after they arrived in the Central Highlands.
There was no medicine for anything.

I often received an embarrassed plea from Diep's sister
Minh for *any* kind of medicine, from aspirin to cold tab-
lets, soothing ointments or vitamins, and my attempts to
hide these treasures inside mailed skeins of yarn—one of
the few items I was allowed to send by the Vietnamese
government—were usually foiled. I would later learn that
the much-needed ''gifts'' had not been received. Several
yards of material, in the ''suitable black or brown shades,
washable,'' were confiscated, too, or else all but a half
foot of material—not enough to make anything—was cut
off.

Of course, any gifts sent to Vietnam had to be sent to
Minh, who would then keep them until Diep or one of her
children came down out of the Central Highlands for a

visit. This usually occurred only twice a year, since the trip took almost three days of steady riding in buses that were not what we consider comfortable passenger vehicles; they were ancient and broke down often.

. . . Many people they have tuberculosis. Some have other parasites which make them die. We work very hard morning to night, because if our crops don't produce good harvest of rice, we won't eat next year. Our food allowance until that crop is due will be spent.

Jolie is so tiny, we laugh at her. My back aches every night from bending all day long, wading in water of rice paddies. Jolie so short she don't have to bend! Next year we work the sugar cane. That is very hard work, too. Very little food, Sister.

Whenever Larry and I attended an "all you can eat" restaurant, the thought occurred to me—and I'd have to let it go quickly—that here we were with the best food, and as much as we could gluttonously consume, and there were people in other parts of the world with barely enough to subsist on.

Diep's letters mentioned her situation, but only in passing.

. . . arms ache from tossing rice in baskets, but we do well with our crops. We fool the Communist leaders when they tell us how much we must produce. I save and hide some rice out, putting the dry rice on the bottom and the top in the Communist boss' barrel, with the damper and heavier rice—NO GOOD!—in the middle. They no discover, and then I give the hungry neighbors a little more food.

. . . I send this letter in care of my sister in Saigon.

It will take a long time, but you receive it and write to me in her care also.

Minh wrote to me asking for help in finding some way to get her and Freddy out of Vietnam. Her letters were frequently sad, as she worried for her handsome son, whose intelligence had attracted the attention of his Communist teachers. The last thing she wanted was for Freddy to be taken away and "trained" for some "higher calling."

Diep later told me about Mr. Lai, an old man who had been a neighbor in Da Nang. She often thought about him when she was in the Central Highlands, wondering how he was faring. He had been abandoned by a very young wife when their two boys were infants. She had run off with another man, and her husband had reared the children to adulthood.

"His sons became very fine men, and they never resented their mother who went off to marry a Vietnamese officer. Mr. Lai was a good person, never married again, and saw his sons finish secondary school. The oldest was in the Hue University, and the second son was my brother's age. Mr. Lai's family was poor when his younger son and my brother were in the service in 1973. They were both officers in the Vietnamese Armed Forces in only nine months after finishing school.

"The war by then was all over South Vietnam. Many soldiers were dying in the battles. Mr. Lai's son, Vinh, after only five months, went to battle in South Vietnam and he was killed in May 1974. He had fallen into the river about thirty miles from Mecong Delta and drowned. He had drowned, not killed honorably in battle, and his poor father contemplated such a waste.

"A telegram arrived telling Mr. Lai about his dead son. DEAR SIR: YOUR SON DIED FOR HIS COUNTRY MAY 19, 1974. PLEASE PICK UP HIS BODY AS SOON AS POSSIBLE, AT KIEN TUONG PROVINCE. I was very sorry for the poor old man. He couldn't cry or even speak. We were his neighbors, so we helped him. I went with him to pick up his son's body, fifteen miles from the Cambodia border, and there were big battles all around. I was very frightened. I did not want to see it, and we came in the daylight around noon. We had taken the bus from Saigon to this province. The rain was coming down heavy and heavier. We searched and asked many questions before finding the place where Vinh's body was held. It was near the gate of the Administry of Vietnamese Armed Forces, and we had to see the body and identify.

"Mr. Lai cried: 'My dear son, you will be here forever. Your soul was always at the battle. I lost you evermore!' He lay down beside the coffin, and I saw hundreds of coffins on shelves one on top of the other. I cried too, louder and louder. One body of a husband had been there one month. The body still waited for his wife to pick up, and I think she was afraid to come alone and claim it.

"I will never forget my sickness that day. The smell from hundreds of dead bodies mixed with incense which they burn to hide it, and the flowers someone saved all around made the smell overpowering me. I went tearfully outside and rested by the gate. A young officer walked up and asked if he could help me.

"I said, 'No, thank you.'

"He said, 'It is sad that so many young, beautiful men must die in this way. I know how you feel.' He gave me a flower. He did not know, but I was not crying for Vinh, and I was not crying for myself. I was crying for Vietnam. I went back inside and saw the hundreds of coffins in the big hall, all in rows with the Vietnam flag on them, and my eyes would not see the yellow color of the flag.

"They put him in a bag and then in coffin, and we took him by truck to Saigon and then to Da Nang."

Since having a proper burial for loved ones is important to the Vietnamese, Diep knew she had done the right thing. She made several such pilgrimages for various friends and neighbors, always with a tender kindness toward people whose suffering was greater than her own.

She later told me how she feigned the pride of a good Communist worker:

"We were schooled to think the Vietnamese women were the heroines of the war, killing Chinese, Americans, and standing up to the freedom for Vietnam, and to practice these beautiful thoughts, I must remain in Central Highlands to make and rebuild the beauty of our country. I would be a good labor person and love the Socialists in the Central Highlands. To practice my beautiful thoughts, I must learn to reform and I would work in the rice, bean, and sugar fields.

"When we had arrived there, it was so cold at night. We didn't have warm clothes anymore. The war had destroyed them. I had never labored by hand and didn't know how to do. No house. No food. I could go without the food, but not my poor children.

"But once again I would win by my mind, I thought. Now I was agricultural leader, and we learned much. I learn how to be good laborer and good Socialist citizen, and sometimes when I was headachy and sleepy, I used to knit to forget the time. Then one day someone saw me knit and became unpleasant. 'You stop knitting,' they said as they taught us how to be good members of the new government.

" 'It is my head that understands your talk,' I told them. 'My hands don't understand anyhow. Let my hands keep busy and labor good.' They left me alone.

"My children were enrolled in the school and learn very much about the politics. They learned about Materialism, Capitalism, Communism. They knew well about Karl Marxism, and they learned better than me. We never talk in English. They say that we should forget anything we know about the American. 'What you say in English?' They tried to trick me. 'I don't know anything in English,' I lied. But after a time, I forget much about English and yet never forget my dream about coming to America!"

Sometimes when North Vietnamese men were in the area, Diep hid her daughters under the bed. The South Vietnamese left her alone, but the North Vietnamese were a threat. Jolie and Jeanie begged her at one point to dye their brown hair as black as her own, but she refused. "Say you're Russian. That is all," she continued to instruct them.

She described digging the irrigation canals herself with the help of her two children and how they made such wonderful sugar when Jolie was "the cow" and turned the masher around its cauldron of sugarcane. Eventually, Jolie was replaced by a real cow, but the child—despite her eighty pounds and five-foot frame—had considerable strength. How exhausted she was when, after four hours in the morning of this work, it was time to go to school. The girls had old bicycles to make the seven-mile trip through slippery wet clay during the heavy monsoon rains. When the bikes broke down, it was Jeanie who was the mechanic.

"If you couldn't fix them," she said matter-of-factly, "you walked." One becomes quite ingenious under these circumstances.

Diep was good at mathematics and learned quickly. When her books did not agree with the boss's books, she managed to beguile him into seeing that she had not made a mistake "intentionally." Sometimes she would be scolded, but they told her she knew how to organize people. Her neighbors trusted her. She kept helping them.

As she told me: "Well, I had their love and confidence. They knew I would help them! I always smiled big smile with the boss, but whenever we steal rice from field or hide something, we look so innocent. They would not say anything, but I think sometimes they knew."

Later Jolie would recall her life in the Central Highlands:

"My mother still had a little money left when we came to Ban Me Thuot, but we were poor, with no house or position in life.

"In April of 1976, my family had no more food to eat. The crop had not come in yet. The famine was threatening the life of my family. I was so hungry. After my mother worked in the field, she would go out and try to find some food for me. I ate anything I could eat: I ate the bud of the banana tree, the leaves of the red pepper tree, and some kinds of weeds that live in the fields.

"After that, my mother tried to borrow some food from some kind neighbors. Those foods were the dry manioc, the kind of food used for pigs before 1975, and for more than one year we did not have the meat or the fish. We tried to get through just until my family had the ripening rice.

"I still remember when I was small child of ten years old. I remember when my mother had to work in the fields from before she came up until long after dark, and when she came home to her one meal at night only to have a bowl of yucky soup. ["Yucky" was one of the first words Jolie learned from Americans.]

"I don't want to remember that time, but I will never be able to forget. Never and never. . . . I felt happy when the school year came to an end. I always got prize for being good student. Because I was Amerasian, and I didn't want my friends to look down on me, I tried to get honors for me and for my mother. I was better student after 1975 than before."

I received several letters that year from Diep or from her sister Minh telling me that the little family suffered from respiratory infections, parasitic infections, and eye disorders. Diep was very frail, I knew, and the thought of her toiling at back-breaking labor in the hot sun—ill and unable to rest—was sometimes more than I could bear to think about.

In June of 1980 Diep wrote me about her health. The tone of her letters was never complaining, merely informational as they asked me for medicine, help that the postal restrictions of Vietnam forbade.

Dear Sister,

I have been very sick. I have trouble working. Jeanie very sick, too. She tried to bring wood from the forest for our firewood we need, and slipped into the river. She nearly drowned, and I was so terrible thinking she was going to die. Then they found her, walking her bicycle home alone in the dark late at night, the wind and rain soaking her more after her bad fall into the river, which try to sweep her away.

Jeanie she got the chills and high fever and bad rattles in her chest. Somebody say she would die. Many people died already from same sickness. We waited until the fever went down a little and put her on the bus for Saigon so she would be with my sister.

It had been during the monsoon season of heavy rains that Jeanie had gone after firewood to keep the sugarcane simmering in the cauldron. She had traveled much farther than she had intended, deep into the forest, and when she discovered two large logs she could not resist tying them to the back of her bicycle. She thought that if she got these logs home, perhaps she would not have to come back for more wood for a day or two.

The clumsy logs dragging behind her bicycle kept throwing her off balance, and as she neared a steep bank overlooking the swiftly moving river below, the logs slid down the bank, dragging her and the overturned bicycle into the rushing current.

She was carried with the logs, one of which hit her on the head. Jeanie was not a strong swimmer. Frantically, she managed to clutch at a tree branch as she was swept by. Hanging on for her life, she painfully pulled herself onto the bank where she lay, coughing and gasping, until she had recovered enough to realize that her precious logs were caught on rocks in the water not far below her. She could not lose them now!

The eighty-five-pound girl managed to go back into the water and work her way to the place where one of the logs was caught on some rocks; working against the current, she pulled it free and back to shore. The bank was as slippery as glass. It was raining heavily and the oozing red mud now forced Jeanie to claw her way with one hand while she pulled the log with the other. Finally she lay exhausted at the top of the bank, her log beside her.

Somehow the determined and plucky girl managed to drag the log, many times the length of her bicycle. "I wasn't going to pay such a price for something and then lose it," she told her mother after the ordeal passed. The same determination compelled Jeanie to repair the bike, which she would have risked her life to save from the current. "Bicycles are most important to Vietnamese people," she explained to me. "I have seen people kill for a bicycle."

Later, at home, Jeanie developed a fever that was raging before Diep found a woman—a nun—who sold them medicine to alleviate it and stave off pneumonia. The girl was so weak and ill that it was decided she should be taken to Saigon to stay with her aunt just as soon as she was out of immediate danger. Diep knew that it would be a long time before Jeanie would be strong enough to return to the arduous work in the Central Highlands.

The duties were now divided between Diep and Jolie, and they accepted the situation in the quiet and resigned way that they accepted most things. In Saigon, Jeanie was determined to make her visit worthwhile. She would attempt to handle the paperwork necessary for her mother's and sister's freedom. If she filled out papers, went through the required interviews, and made it sound as if her mother were illiterate and stupid, it was possible they might receive their exit visas out of Vietnam.

She worried that when the time came for her mother to be interviewed by the Communist officials, Diep might appear to be smarter and more capable than Jeanie had described her. The application and the applicant had to match.

During the year and a half that Jeanie stayed with her

aunt Minh and cousin Freddy, she went to school in Saigon and developed the street sense and survival instincts that most children there had to learn, particularly the Amerasian children. She and Freddy however, were much luckier than most other Amerasian children since they had a home, to say nothing of mothers who loved and accepted them.

One day an American journalist came to the city to photograph Amerasian children. As people crowded around him, Freddy rushed quickly through the throng and thrust a note into the startled man's hand. The note beseeched him to find Freddy's father, saying that food was scarce and that Freddy yearned to meet his father. [An amusing sidelight to this: The American had a very hairy chest, which greatly impressed the boy, and when Freddy returned home he told his mother that if he had a chest like that, he would never be cold again.]

Now that her sister was not there to help, Jolie was having a difficult time, especially since it was Jeanie who was the resident mechanic. When the bike broke down, Jolie, whose talents were in areas other than mechanics, had to struggle to fix it herself.

Jeanie wrote to her mother on several occasions telling her to be cheerful, and that there was a good possibility they would be granted exit visas. Jeanie had a singleness of purpose in checking with the city officials on a regular basis. "Of course, I never believed she would succeed," Diep told me later.

"When I think about those little girls in the Central Highlands working so hard every day *after* fourteen miles round trip to and from school on a rickety bike, it makes me realize how lucky my own children are," I told Dottie at lunch one afternoon.

"She'll never get out with her kids, you know," Dottie said softly. "She's there for life." She gave me a level stare, a look that defied any challenge.

"I don't believe that. I can't give up on her."

"You'd better start believing," Dottie said authoritatively. "You're so bull-headed and stubborn, but clinging to the hope that you can get her out is self-torture. As long as she's useful to them, they'll keep her there."

I smiled. "Well, you know me. I never give up on something that's really important to me."

"You just don't know when to quit, do you? Look, Janni, why don't you save yourself the frustration. It's beginning to look like an obsession, you know. Let her go. Just let her go."

"I can't. It's not even a consideration."

But I wondered if Dottie was right. My life was hardly dull. I was teaching part time at the college, teaching piano lessons twenty hours a week, and tutoring up to six hours a day for the school district. My children were teenagers now, and we were a close family. My life was filled with activity and people I loved. Why, I wondered, was this bond with Nguyen Thi Diep, thousands of miles away and virtually a stranger to me, so strong? Why did I feel so emotionally involved in her life, her fate?

Writing *Child in the White Fog* had been a necessary part of my own healing process, but I discovered other "therapies" as well. I volunteered for the local chapter of the National Cystic Fibrosis Foundation, as did Larry, and together we found many ways we could put our knowledge about this dreaded disorder to work.

Both of us discovered a much-needed sense of community and purpose, a feeling grief often obliterates. I believe that our experiences in life—especially the hurtful ones—impart a responsibility to use their lessons and to share them in every way possible.

When I scheduled speaking engagements on cystic fibrosis throughout northern California, I discovered yet another outlet for the lingering pain of my Marna's death. At the end of each talk people often asked personal questions.

"Do you still fall apart on occasion?" a young mother asked me during the refreshment period one evening. Larry overheard her question as he stood nearby but said nothing. I looked at him and asked, "Do I?" He smiled and nodded.

"Yes," I said, turning back to her. "I suspect that the 'soggies' will always get me when I least expect them. They can overtake me while I'm driving somewhere and a certain song is played over the radio. Or the blooming of the camellia tree outside the window will remind me . . . or I'll pass by Marna's photograph and suddenly see those dark eyes looking out at me, and I'll dissolve into a bath of tears."

"I fixed a little pillow-seat on the handlebars of my bike for Marni to sit on when I took her for a ride," Larry said. "She loved to go for rides. Well, the other day I spotted it crumpled up in the corner of the tool shed where I had tossed it after she . . ." He paused. "It was nothing more than a few rags rolled up, yet I couldn't really throw it away."

He smiled and shook his head. "I guess it helps to have a sense of humor and the ability to laugh at yourself. It helps get you over those dark periods."

The woman's rapt face and sad eyes conveyed that she was currently experiencing her own "dark periods."

"Perhaps if I became really busy. I suppose that I've

just been hiding away from the world," she said falteringly.

"Activity can be a wonderful healer," I said. "And if that activity is in some way connected with the source of the pain, it is even more effective."

"When I think about the tremendous suffering of mothers all over the country who are losing their sons in Vietnam, I'm humbled," the woman said. "I mean, think of how many thousands of parents have been told that their young sons, often just beginning to live their lives, have been killed in that senseless war!"

"Well, the Vietnamese losses are heavy, too," her husband chimed in.

"It's *their* war, just the same," she replied. "I can't be too sympathetic."

I thought about Diep, whose one brother had taken his life in despair, whose other brother fought in a war that terrified him and played havoc with his very sanity, whose home had been taken, along with all of her possessions, who worked at hard labor with her two daughters ten to sixteen hours a day. This was hardly Diep's war, any more than it was mine!

That night I wrote a letter on Diep's behalf to Congressman George Miller, a letter that finally after all those years, would make a difference. It was not unlike a hundred I had composed before, but the phone call that came in response to it marked the beginning of Diep's dream coming true.

Chapter Eight

"My Sister, She Get Out of Vietman!"

I decided to post my letter to Congressman Miller on my way to my substitute teaching assignment at Northridge High School. As I pulled over to a mailbox next to a gas station, a nicely dressed man in a late-model sports car asked me directions to the school. Before I could answer, two boys overheard and started to walk toward his car.

"Northridge? Y'mean Northridge Prison?" One of them laughed. "Yeah, we're inmates, man," he said as he pointed up the road.

"Inmates?" his friend said kiddingly. "Shit, we're escapees." He bent over to light his cigarette, shielding the match from the dry September wind as his long, straw-colored hair fell over his forehead. Then they jumped into a new Toyota and screeched off, the car's stereo blare fading into the distance.

The approach to Northridge High School leads past manicured lawns and gardener-tended flowerbeds. The expensive homes represent every architectural style from Tudor to Spanish colonial, all set beneath the sentinel watch of Mt. Diablo.

On that particular morning as I parked in the faculty lot, I looked at Northridge and thought how this grand "prison for the privileged" might look to the two little Vietnamese girls who labored so far away in the Central Highlands of Vietnam. As they toiled in the sugarcane fields and rice paddies, desiring above all else their freedom and an education, what would they think about the two cynical boys in the Toyota? They would never understand.

While I waited for a response from Congressman Miller, I was offered a new professional challenge. I was interviewed for a teaching position in a psychiatric hospital.

"This might be a difficult assignment," said Robert Bettemann, the supervisor for the Home and Hospital Special Services Program, which had employed me part time for several years. Until now, my assignments had always been short term, taking me to homes and hospitals when students were too ill to attend school. I was a tutor of any subject commonly taught in grades seven through twelve.

"Many of these kids will be heavily medicated, and some are barely capable of learning anything. Remember, this is an acute facility."

"Meaning?"

"These kids are severely disturbed, many of them. Some are suicidal. Some are even homicidal. Think you can handle it?"

"When do I start?"

"I'll call Julie LaPrez, the education director. You'll have to earn her endorsement, but have no worry about that."

The privately owned psychiatric hospital was at the end of a narrow road, which provided access to medical offices and to the back entrance of the emergency room of a large medical hospital. This community hospital was the first step for suicidal patients before they were admitted to the psychiatric facility, which could handle about three hundred patients.

The main lobby was intended to resemble a living room, with overstuffed sectional couches and potted plants, which, when driven to explore their lush foliage, I discovered to be artificial. The receptionist asked my purpose without meeting my gaze, then made the call for Mrs. LaPrez and disappeared.

While I waited, an elderly woman dressed in a robe and slippers walked into the lobby and sat down next to me. A cigarette hung from her lower lip as she conversed with the doctor who had followed her in. He was slowly and carefully explaining to her how her daughter and son-in-law would be taking her home on a weekend pass, and what was expected of her. He patiently went over the directions on the bottles of medication he had given to her. I watched her fumble with the bottles and place them in a crocheted purse, and I sensed her nervousness as the doctor said good-bye to her and left.

She sat staring at the door for a minute, then turned to me. "You a new admission?" she asked.

"No," I replied.

"I think you're lying," she said in a matter-of-fact way. "Everyone's always lying about it.

"Who put you in here?" she persisted.

"I'm a visitor," I told her, wishing her daughter would come.

"I think you're lying," she said again. She looked sideways at me. "You got any smokes for me?"

I told her that I did not.

"I'm all out," she said, feeling in her robe pockets. "You got a match? That'd be a start."

I apologized for not having a match either.

"I think you have matches," she said after a long pause. *"Everyone's* got matches!"

I realized that I would now be operating in a very different world from any I had dealt with before, but I believed that some of my life experiences made me particularly suited to work with troubled people because I was successfully conquering some demons of my own.

Julie LaPrez appeared, a woman in her early thirties with intense blue eyes that seemed to take in much more than they focused on. She sized me up for a moment, then led me into her office.

"Have you any credentials?" she asked.

I nodded. "A secondary credential and a junior college credential."

"This position has stressful moments," she said. "Not everyone can handle it, but Robert sent you over with high recommendations. He tells me you've worked with the Pregnant Minor Program."

"Yes," I replied. "A much-needed program, too."

"Robert says you've taught in juvenile hall. What was that like?"

"Challenging," I told her, "and taxing and rewarding, too."

"How so?"

"I felt needed. I related well to teenagers, and besides, it was the only teaching job I could find immediately after graduating from college. I began as a substitute teacher-counselor, but it turned into something more full time. I have been doing this for nearly two years now, in addition to substitute teaching for three school districts."

"This assignment would be at least five hours a day and just as stressful as your work at the Hall," Julie told me. "You probably won't have much time for other teaching work when you work here. Were you ever fearful when you were working at the Hall?"

"No, not at all. At first I merely tutored kids on a one-on-one basis, so I became comfortable with the environment quickly. It wasn't until I had been there a few months that they had me teach in the classrooms."

"Do the teachers still wear the classroom key around their necks, with a guard posted outside the classroom door?"

"Yes." I smiled. "But I never had to call him."

She studied my face for a moment, then asked: "Would you like to tour the hospital?" I nodded.

The quarters of West Wing and North Wing resembled hotel rooms off each long corridor, with nurses' stations at either end. Patients came and went freely, but they were not allowed out of their individual wings without an escort. As Julie and I strolled down the corridor, younger patients greeted her; I was impressed with her compassionate manner, her strength and calmness.

"Julie," a blue-jacketed technician called out as we passed one of the nursing stations, "Wanda Ramsey has been missing since lunch. You haven't seen her, have you?"

"No. Have you searched the recreation room?"

"Nancy and Tom are there now, but no word so far."

Julie turned to me. "Sometimes that happens," she said. "A patient will just take off, but they usually come back."

"Where will she go without money?" I asked.

"She might have had some friend from the outside help her, or she might have hitchhiked somewhere—perhaps to her grandmother's. Her parents are alcoholics, separated, and the girl has lived most of her life with her grandparents."

My expression must have conveyed something to Julie.

She stopped. "You can't let the stories get to you," she said softly. "You're pretty sensitive, I can tell, and that's good. But it can get in your way when you work in a place like this."

"Mr. Bettemann said that most of the students are on medication."

"That's right. Even when they can't focus or concentrate, the doctors agree that schooling is a vital part of their therapy. We just do the best we can. As they get better, we can do more and more."

At the other end of the hallway in the closed unit I spotted a woman being brought in by the back door. Far from being subdued, she yelled obscenities at her captors, who now held her tightly. I realized this was the missing Wanda. Suddenly she struggled free and rushed toward us. Two technicians caught her, pinned her arms behind her back, and forced her into a nearby wheelchair.

"They'll probably place her in four-point restraints," Julie told me. "That means she'll have her wrists and ankles strapped either to the chair, or . . ."

I followed her gaze. Wanda was being wheeled into a room with a euphemistic sign above the door: *QUIET ROOM*.

"Now she can scream to her heart's content," an attendant observed to us. "No one can hear her now."

"When will she get out?" I asked Julie.

"After she's had her medication and calmed down. When patients are violent or especially under stress, four-point restraints actually calm them down. Sometimes it's the only way that we can administer medication."

Teenagers and elderly patients strolled, paced, or shuffled up and down the corridor that extended to the locked doors of West Wing. Some clasped their hands behind them, some moved with an uncertain stumbling, drugged gait like blind people without cane or dog.

Those who sat in wheelchairs just stared at us; a few reached out to touch us as we passed. Many were absorbed in a distant world we could not see, talking to people visible only to them.

Julie explained about the written reports required of all teachers at the end of each school day. She described the students' schedules, their exercise programs, and their group therapy sessions: "You may attend these if you like. There will be an 11 A.M. group meeting, which I'll want you to sit in on daily."

She had a list of "nevers" and a brief rundown on staff and personnel. The daily 11:00 A.M. "rap session" for teachers and their students was an opportunity for reviews where both the kids and their instructors could compare notes and even air their frustrations, if need be. The one-on-one tutoring necessitated the use of journals kept by the students, she said, since the head psychiatrist believed fervently in such things.

"You impress me as a compassionate person," she said as she leaned far back in her swivel chair, arms behind her head. Her blue eyes studied my face intently. "That compassion and caring are sorely needed in a place like this. Love—enough of it, I think—can cut through just about anything." There was a long pause. "Do you have any questions you'd like to ask me, Jann?"

"No," I said, momentarily distracted by a stocky boy of about seventeen who shouted at a nurse to give him a cigarette. As I watched, he suddenly vaulted over the counter into the nurses' station, his arm raised as if to hit the woman. Two male attendants, who had been talking nearby, promptly jumped him. A brief struggle ensued, punctuated by the boy's screamed obscenities, as he was held down and placed in restraints.

"That's Tony," Julie said calmly. "He's always belligerent. He'll also be one of your students."

Tony was tied to his wheelchair and brought to me in the closed unit classroom that first day. He refused to look at me, staring instead at his knees.

"I brought you a new notebook," I began tentatively, trying to sound cheerful. He said nothing and just continued to stare at his knees.

"Your doctor told me that you'd really like to keep up with your studies," I said lamely.

"He's a prick," Tony muttered.

"Well, I wouldn't know about that."

"He's an asshole." Tony tried again.

"If you say so," I ventured. "Now, about your . . ."

"So are you!" He looked up and stared at me, challenging me with his eyes. I said nothing and showed no response at all, beyond staring calmly back at him. "Did you hear me?" he raised his voice threateningly.

"Yes, I did, Tony. But why don't you reserve your judgment about me until you know me?" I picked up the math book he was to use. He waited for me to say something else, tensed as if ready to fight. I saw that his fists were clenched in spite of the fact that his wrists were tied to the sides of the chair.

"You can't teach me that crap!" he said, staring down at his knees again.

"Your school counselor said that math was your best subject, Tony."

"Yeah, well that was before I got into Mr. Clemmer's math class."

"Well, I have a confession: Math was my poorest subject."

He looked up, startled. "Then how come you're teaching it?"

"Good question. It's pretty hard to find teachers who have expertise in *all* subjects."

"You mean I might have to tutor *you?*" There was a tinge of humor in his question, and the hostility subsided for a moment.

"Yes, that's possible." I smiled. "Are you a good tutor?"

"How much'll you pay me?" he asked sardonically.

"How much do you want?"

"A pack of smokes for every tutoring session." He tested me.

"Sorry. But I *can* manage an occasional Baskin-Robbins cone."

"Jamoca Almond Fudge?"

"Deal!"

Fortunately for me, Tony's math that semester consisted of geometry, a subject easier than algebra for me, so I didn't owe him many ice cream cones. Since Tony was a repeater—that is, a patient who found it safer to be locked up in the hospital than to remain on the outside—he returned within weeks of every release, and he always asked for me as his teacher.

Then one afternoon I overheard one of the nurses discussing Tony with a doctor. "He overdid things this time," she said. "I hear he got some angel dust and ended up at Napa."

"He's scrambled," the young technician standing near

them added. ''Too bad, 'cause I think Tony was basically a bright kid, just so self-destructive.''

That semester I encountered many other sad young people. I would gladly have ''adopted'' them all. There were three fifteen-year-old girls who had committed every backlash at society imaginable, yet I saw genuinely wonderful qualities in them. One of these girls I'll call Heather. She had never known who her father was. Her mother was an alcoholic who was violently abusive when she was not passed out. Over the years, Heather had been sexually attacked by two of her mother's male friends. She had been picked up the first time for soliciting when she was only twelve years old and, in addition to numerous arrests, had a long record of visits to Juvenile Hall as a runaway.

The first time I saw her was the morning after she had swallowed a bottle of Seconal that her boyfriend had given her to sell for him. She was dazed and ill, having had her stomach pumped, but was otherwise all right.

''You don't look like you're in any shape for a tutoring session,'' I said good-naturedly.

She tossed back her long, thick dark hair and looked defiantly at me, studying my face carefully. ''You want to get out of teaching me?'' she asked with a smile.

''Not really,'' I said. ''Do you feel okay?''

''Not really.''

''Can I get you something?''

She looked a bit startled, then said, ''My mother. They won't let me see her.'' I detected a catch in her voice, but she held her head high and stared at me suspiciously.

''Does your mother know you're here?''

''Of course she does.''

''You want me to call her and ask her to come?''

''I want you to call her and *demand* she come!''

''To have you released?''

''NO! I don't want to go home, not yet.'' Her voice broke, and there was a little sob as she looked away from me. ''Never mind. My mom wouldn't make it down here anyway. I was just testing you.''

''You don't have to do that,'' I told her. ''I'm in your corner.''

''You don't know what my corner looks like,'' she said softly.

''Yeah, you're probably right.''

She glanced at me hastily, defiance, pain, and confusion in her large green eyes. What a pretty girl, I thought. What a waste.

''They won't let me go back home this time,'' she said, trying to fight the tears. ''The court'll send me to some foster home.''

''It might not be so bad.''

''Yeah? Well, that's what *you* know about it. I hear that some foster parents are mean and make you work in spite of the fact that they get paid to keep kids. I know one guy who got beaten all the time by his foster dad.''

''Is that what you're afraid of?''

''No. I've been beaten before. I just want to go home.''

''It's been decided that your home is not the best place for you, Heather.''

She turned away from me again. ''I want . . . I want . . . to die,'' she said in a little-girl voice.

''I don't want you to die,'' I told her, wondering if I could touch her, comfort her; but she sat rigid, closed within herself.

''Have you ever wanted to die?'' she asked at last, not looking at me. I could tell by the shudder of her shoulders that she was weeping silently. The tone of her voice indicated that she was sure that this was another ''corner'' I knew nothing about.

"Yes, I *have* wanted to give up on life," I said simply.

"Why?" She turned to show a tear-streaked face, but one that also had a bright curiosity.

"Because there was so much pain in my life I wanted to escape from it," I said. She nodded in understanding.

"Then why didn't you end it?"

"Because . . . because there was something inside me that loved life more, and I'm really not a quitter after all. I like myself better for hanging on and fighting the pain."

"Yeah, I guess I know what you mean," she said.

Driving home I thought about the desperation that drives people to end their lives, the terrible emptiness that precedes such a final decision. I thought about my friend in Vietnam who had witnessed some friends and neighbors abandon the struggles and sorrows of living, whose own brother had chosen death over the agony of life. I thought about how Diep herself had finally chosen life with all of its uncertainties and pain and promise.

Of course, Diep and her children supported each other with a deep, abiding love that Heather had never known.

That evening I told Larry about Heather. I had been going through a box of Marna's dresses, which I had never been able to get rid of and only now could consider sending to a children's shelter. The familiar sorrow stopped me, and I said, "Would you ever consider being a foster parent to a kid like Heather? I mean, since Marna's death . . ."

Larry got up from his chair and walked into the bathroom without a word. I followed, since he had left the door open. He was just standing there, his hands on the sink as if to steady himself. "I guess we could," he said in a choked voice.

Then I thought about the four children watching television in the next room, children who had known a lifetime of more than a few little upsets and some deprivation themselves. "Oh, Honey," I told Larry, "your kindness is appreciated, but I guess that's not such a good idea, is it?"

I would never forget his willingness to at least consider taking on another child, especially since someone like Heather would have been one of the biggest challenges we could ever have faced.

I worked with her for several months. Every time her doctor thought she was well enough to be released to the people who had been selected to take her, Heather did something that forced her doctor to keep her hospitalized. Once she hit one of the technicians hard enough to require stitches. Another time she overdosed; she had somehow managed to save her medication instead of swallowing it, until she had enough pills to make her quite ill.

Then one day I came to work and Heather wasn't there. I was told she had learned that her mother had been severely beaten and was near death in a hospital about eighty miles away.

Julie LaPrez filled me in: "I didn't want you to hear this from anyone else, but someone must have told Heather rather bluntly about her mom, not expecting much of a reaction. Well, Heather took off crying."

"What do you mean she took off?" I wanted to know.

"She's gone. No one has any idea where she is."

"When did this happen?"

"On your day off. I would have said something earlier to you, but I hoped Heather would return before I got everyone upset. Anyhow, I don't think there's much hope she'll come back now."

She never did.

Julie was right.

That terrible let down was somewhat counterbalanced by a little action on Diep's behalf.

Dear Mrs. Jansen:

I am Congressman George Miller's assistant, and he asked me to get back to you regarding the letter you sent him about the Nguyen family. The problem, as you may already know, lies more with Vietnam in not allowing their people to leave. Once they are granted exit visas, it is not so difficult gaining entrance to the USA. Now, I suggest you contact Mrs. Pat Waltermire of the Northern California and Nevada Refugee Sponsorship Service. She is the current director, and can advise you better than I.

Sincerely,
Mrs. Carol Pollard
September 17, 1980

I received an encouraging call on September 20, 1980.

"Mrs. Jansen? This is Pat Waltermire. Carol Pollard from Congressman Miller's office told me about you and your friends in Vietnam. I want to set up an appointment with you and see how we might help you get them out of Vietnam." The warmth and confidence in Pat Waltermire's voice filled me with the first hope I had had in all of the years since I realized that Diep and I had a strong bond between us. Perhaps at last I had found someone who could be of help.

The meeting with Mrs. Waltermire on September 24th left me discouraged once again. She seemed disappointed too. Her compassion for the refugees was undeniable.

"It's a dreadful situation," she said. "We would accept many more refugees than Vietnam will release. If your friend worked for our government, and if she is fluent in English, who knows how they are treating her? I wish I could be more encouraging, but we'll take down the information you can supply and send it on to the Orderly Departure Program secretary.''

''Don't despair,'' she said as I got up to leave. She must have seen the expression on my face. ''These things take time. I know you've already been hoping for her release for many years, but we've seen many success stories here, too.''

With the promise that we would keep in touch, I left. All the way home I told myself that I was doing everything I could. Dottie's prophesy that Diep and her children were ''lifers'' in Vietnam's agricultural New Economic Zone was something I would not accept.

Dear Mrs. Jannice, my sister,

The Vietnamese wear the old uniforms of the Vietnam soldier. Once I see the movie in Saigon called ''Bridge over the River Kwai,'' and we look like the people in the movie very much.

I spent one hundred and twenty days in the woods this time digging the water irrigation for a big stream to lead it to the field for our rice plantation. I have worked very hard for four months. Now I work with group to produce rice and am still bookkeeper. I cheat when I find that the green beans are sold to Russia and the poor Vietnamese need very much and go hungry. Tet is coming, and so I keep some green beans out for us and have the people harvest some green beans on Saturday for themselves. The government people come and tell us to harvest on Sunday, not know about my cheating.

Well, someone want a favor from them and tell about my cheat. They say I must make report. I went to each house and warned people to lie, and they all say we didn't take more beans. When New Year Tet comes, we must have sticky rice, beans and meat. Then we go into the dark night and harvest rice, and the government men not know. We are so hungry, and my children work so hard just for little bit of food. . . .

Diep

"Isn't she afraid that her letter will be read?" my daughter Donice wanted to know.

"Only the mail going in to Vietnam seems to be tampered with, perhaps because the authorities are confiscating contraband or items they can sell on the black market," I said. "I'll write her and tell her to be more careful about what she writes. There have been letters with holes cut out, so some of the outgoing mail *is* censored. She must be warned. It just isn't worth it. There isn't much value placed on human life there anyhow, and she could be used as an example and punished."

Dearest Sister,

At last I receive permission to get my mother's bones from where she die and take them home to bury again. I had long bus trip from Central Highlands, Ban Me Thuot, to Nha Trang, and was very dusty tired when I get home.

I had some money from knitting sweaters for people in Ban Me Thuot and gave to man who unbury my mother and clean the bones for me. He wrap my mother's bones in sack carefully, and I started for Da Nang.

No one want to give me ride. Bad luck, they say. So I tell no one else what is in sack, and found a bus driver. Each checkpoint, I get scared, since the police would ask what is in bag. If bus driver know, he not let me ride, and I can not walk so far to Da Nang.

Finally a policeman at a checkpoint made us get off the bus, and he ask me what is in bag. I start to cry, and handed him a note telling him it was my mother's body bones and I was taking her home to family burial ground in Da Nang, and please not to say anything.

He was kind to me, and I rode on bus all but ten miles from Da Nang. There I finally put my mother's bones back in the earth for her eternity.

I can feel the peace now that it is done. . . .

                                        Diep

It is a cliché to talk about life dealing us a certain hand, as from a deck of cards, but I often pondered over the disparities between some rich families whose children I tutored, families wealthy in material luxuries but poverty-stricken in love and solid values, and my Vietnamese "sister" whose personal wealth was in her unselfish love for her children and the honor she imparted to them.

Todd's story underscored this difference for me. Todd Remington, a boy I had worked with, was being discharged from the psychiatric hospital against his doctor's advice. His stay had been traumatic for everyone. He was rebellious, volatile, and inclined to bully other teenagers. At seventeen he stood over six feet tall and weighed nearly two hundred pounds.

When he was first admitted, it was for a drug overdose. As a patient, Todd had managed to acquire drugs from visitors or from people who smuggled in packages at night, and he had even supplied some of the most severely psychotic patients for a "reasonable fee."

Todd was one of the most difficult students I was assigned to tutor. He was brilliant, self-confident, and manipulative. He came from a broken home, but in spite of the divorce his father remained close and attentive. The battle between his parents was part of Todd's problem. I had never witnessed two people who hated each other so intensely, so publicly, and with so little regard for the boy whom they used as a pawn between them.

"Jann, the Remingtons wondered if the district would allow a visiting tutor at the home, on a short-term basis, just until he gets back into school full time? Can you manage it?" Bettemann's voice had a plaintive tone. "No one else is interested once they learn something of the kid's history. Besides, you've been working with him for several months now, and he asked for you specifically."

I met with his new counselors at the high school, was given his assignments for biology, English, history, and intermediate algebra, and then headed for the Remington home.

The house was surrounded by a brick and concrete wall with an iron gate. On the wrought-iron arch above the gate, I read: *WORLD OF REMINGTON* in brass letters.

I drove down the private road lined with giant elms, eucalyptus, maple, and pine trees until I caught sight of Spanish roof tiles among the trees. The white stucco and adobe house looked quite old, but the immaculate grounds and trimmed hedges appeared to have daily attention.

As I pulled into the circular driveway in front of the house, Pavarotti was in the middle of a beautiful aria on my new tape. I sat for a minute listening, enjoying the beauty of the Remingtons' garden. I finally removed the key from the ignition, interrupting Pavarotti on a high clear note, and got out of the car.

A tile fountain, adorned by a dozen marble cupids doing rude things in unison, stood in the middle of the carpet-like lawn. Enormously fat Koi swam lazily beneath the surface of the water as I dipped my hand into the clear coolness of the fountain. Mt. Diablo, in the distance, was the only thing visible from where I stood that was not part of Remington's World, the only other intruder besides me in this isolated scene.

I rang the doorbell and heard a series of chimes inside. A uniformed maid, starchly formal from her crisp, white cap to her black, polished shoes, answered unsmilingly. She left me standing inside as she disappeared to announce my arrival.

I stood and gazed at the open inner courtyard before me, which appeared like a garden of brilliant-colored flowers and bird baths beneath the blue sky. The main house was about forty feet in front of me, with another set of iron gates and another brick pathway, which led out of sight. Gigantic philodendrons and fern grew amid dense moss and baby tears along the banks of a clear-running stream, which appeared to flow unimpeded beneath the arched bridge near the front door and proceed through the house.

The midday sun sent its rays through the ten-foot skylights overhead. Azaleas, rhododendrons, and potted orchids lined the path down which the maid had vanished. As I was taking in the beauty of this unreal place, she reappeared and motioned me to follow, without speaking.

I was met by a tall woman with frosted blond hair and deeply lined, tanned skin, which seemed glued to her prominent bones. She extended her hand with its long, squared-off sculptured nails. "Mrs. Jansen? I am Todd's mother."

Mrs. Remington was truly in her world here. Gracefully, like the mannequins who walk the ramps in fashion shows, she swung the flowing sleeves of her Hawaiian print Angel-mu. "We must talk before you meet Todd."

We crossed the polished emerald-green tiles and went through several arched doorways, then entered a huge room lined with bookcases that held no books. A massive fireplace with a raised hearth stood at one end of the room and extended upward to the twelve-foot ceiling. White chairs, lavishly decorated with silk print pillows that looked as if they had not been touched since the day they had been unpacked, circled the fireplace. She motioned me to sit down in a leather chair by a window.

"I have picked up all of the assignments from Todd's high school," I told her. "His teachers only know that he was hospitalized, but it isn't necessary for them to—"

"Know that he's been in an asylum?" she finished my sentence.

I stopped, but only for the moment.

"Mrs. Remington, it was a hospital where—"

"Let's not beat around the bush," she said, not unkindly. "My son has been doing drugs for a long time now, ever since he was in the sixth grade, in fact. As soon as he returns to school he'll get back in with the wrong crowd again, and we'll be right back where we are today— only worse. Home tutoring's the answer!"

"He has been enrolled in a different high school, hasn't he?" I asked her.

"They're all the same. The private schools aren't any better, either. And, from what Todd says, he *really* likes *you!*"

"I thought . . . I mean, I was led to believe that my tutoring was only temporary, until Todd returned."

"I had to tell them that at the school district," she said. "Otherwise they wouldn't have assigned a tutor to the job."

"After a few weeks, they'll cut it off anyhow," I told her.

"We'll see about that. In the meantime, how old are you?"

"What?"

"Your age. How old are you?" When I didn't answer she said, "About thirty? Thirty-five? What?"

"I assure you I'm qualified."

"I know you're a qualified tutor for all those academic subjects, but are you qualified as a lover for my son?"

Suddenly I had the dizzy dreamlike sensation that I was back in the hospital with one of the patients, only this was not a dream. This was real.

"Now, don't look so shocked. If I'm to keep my son from returning to school, I must provide for all of his needs. The doctor keeps him on Thorazine and sleeping pills; you can check off assignments he has supposedly completed and provide him with the . . . other tutoring he will need in the future as well."

I just sat there saying nothing, wondering which doorway was the quickest route to the main exit.

"Naturally, I'm prepared to pay you quite well for your services." That was all I heard as I retreated through the maze of hallways and managed to find myself out in the cooling, clean air of the garden.

I reported all this to Bettemann and he instructed his secretary to void the application for Todd's "home-tutoring." Later I learned that Mrs. Remington had found her son a tutor from another district.

If unreality prevailed where Todd was concerned, I was daily aware of the realities of Diep's world.

Dear Sister Diep,

Your sister's last letter states that the medicines and vitamins that I sent were received. I hope by now you and your girls have been able to benefit from them. The

restrictions from Vietnam against our sending medicines
might get you in trouble, or my packages to you might
be stolen. I always worry about that.

Yes, I still wish to sponsor you. I am once again writing to the people at the Orderly Departure offices requesting their help. Please don't give up. Know that one
day we shall meet, and that your girls will have the fu-
tures you dream for them.

Jann

Shortly thereafter, I received a letter that made me realize that Diep was abandoning hope.

Dearest Sister, hello,

Today I came down to this city Saigon (I shall always
call it Saigon all my life) from Central Highlands. I am
so glad to hear from you and know that you still won't
forget me here. I am so emotion and my tears were over
your kindness and your loves going to us over here! I let
you know how we do appreciate your gifts to us, but
most of all your loves.

My children grow up. They are so cute and so smart.
I feel that I go to the graveyard soon. I am growing so
old, Sister. I have tried to do my best for my dear children. They have to work so hard after they go to school.
I sometimes feel so guilty that I not send them away
when I could. They might be with you now if I had done
the right thing.

I want to write you a long, long letter very much, so
you will understand me.

You brought me the warmness to my heart. Sometimes I felt I lost my soul and my mind, and my spirit
say that you are there for me and my children. I want
to send you my new picture, but I am afraid to have you

see me look this way, and I am afraid to see it, too. The time has taken the youth away.

Thank you for your picture in the *ao dai* Vietnamese dress. It looks so nice on you. You still beautiful and no change ever.

I wonder if I have sinned and God does not forgive me for something. I always pray one day in the future we meet, dear Sister, but now I can not hold on to the dream much longer. It is like the little bird, so quick to fly away with no nest to hold it. You are the sweet heart and so kind, never to forget us in this place. When I work hard and my body ache and hurt, I remember that you are there. . . .

I wept as I read her letter, feeling engulfed by a wave of emptiness and hopelessness which had come and gone so many times over the many years we had corresponded. Why had this stranger come into my life if I could do nothing to help her? As was often the case when I felt such sadness about Diep, my next thoughts were of my own little girl. Why, I wondered, do we have children if we are only going to lose them? These were questions that would never be answered, I realized, but even so, that knowledge did not silence them.

I kept in touch with Mrs. Waltermire, who had become a true friend, and I continued to write letters to various agencies, but my attempts began to slow down as I sensed Diep's despair. All reports regarding the likelihood of her ever getting out of Vietnam were negative. She did not have family already over here. She did not have an American husband who would send for her. Her children did not have an American father who would claim them. She was lost to me and to the world as well. Her talk about "going to the graveyard soon" really disturbed me. This was uncharacteristic of her, and it made me wonder if she were ill.

My piano student was already practicing in the family room when I rushed in, ten minutes late, and spotted the letter with the Vietnamese stamps and familiar handwriting lying on the mail tray. These days a sense of dread accompanied my reading of Diep's letters. If I received a letter from her sister Minh it was even worse, for I always feared that she would be the bearer of some terrible news.

I left the letter unopened and tried to put it out of my mind while I worked with my student, who was practicing Beethoven's Pathétique Sonata for a piano recital set for the following week.

When he left, I picked up Diep's letter and read it, the strains from Beethoven still singing in my head.

My Dearest Sister Jannice,

. . . I came down to see my sister Minh for first time in fifteen months now. It was difficult for transportation, wait in long long line to buy the ticket. I sell more sweaters for the money. People give me what they can to buy the yarn, and I make the pretty sweater for a little more money.

Thank you again for the material you sent me. We make clothes and need them much. Please send us medicine for flu if you can. We have no medicine for anything, and working in water and rice paddies all day we get sick and not get well.

Sister, once again I lose my decision to come to the United States. I met an old friend here. Her family is rich. They not lose anything when the Communist government come in. Well, she and her family pay my way and my girls, but I am here alone and my girls are in

Central Highlands. It take too long to go back and get them. I lose my chance, and maybe not have another like this ever again. My friend, she go by boat, leave at night. Police didn't catch them.

  If ever I have another chance, I will write you. Please give my regards to your children and Mr. Larry.

Diep
March 24, 1981

I mailed Diep several skeins of yarn with plastic bottles of aspirin buried inside each skein, hoping that they would pass Vietnam's postal authorities' inspection. There was no written response from Diep, and later I learned that she never received this package. I tried to send vitamins, too, and these were also "lost."

Dear Diep,

  I hope this arrives before you leave your sister's house. The people at the embassy advised me against trying to send you any more money. It will never reach you, they said. However, I beg you not to give up. Please keep telling yourself that dreams do come true, that prayers are really answered. Please, dear Sister, don't ever think that I will forget you. I'm here, and one day soon you will be, too. And *please* don't try to come by boat. *Too dangerous!*

Jann
July 14, 1981

Although my message remained the same in letter after letter, I no longer believed my own words. I wanted to keep her morale high, if possible, but I couldn't believe the words of hope I offered her. My new fear was that she would try to escape in a clandestine manner and be lost at sea like so many others.

My workload, meanwhile, was beginning to tell on me. The migraine headaches, which had subsided, were now returning with frightening regularity. When an elderly male patient in the closed unit urinated on my new shoes and I cried, I realized that it was time to leave the hospital. My shell was penetrated at last, and with this burnout I lost my effectiveness as a teacher.

"I wish you'd change your mind," Julie said when I announced my decision to leave.

"You're doing too much, as usual," Robert Bettemann counseled. "Between your college classes, the hospital teaching, and your piano lessons, you have the equivalent of three part-time jobs. How about returning to regular home tutoring again, where you'd have fewer hours and more cooperative students? We could sure use your talents. You'd simply be changing to our regular tutoring staff."

"I don't know . . ."

"We have a student who has a brain tumor. . . ."

Something told me to let that one go, to avoid placing myself in another painful situation again. After all, my better judgment advised, you have nothing to prove. You already know that you're capable of dealing with pain. Let someone else handle this. It will be easier to return to home tutoring, where you can arrange your own schedule and take only the number of students you feel you can handle. Let the really difficult cases go to someone else.

Nonetheless, the next morning I visited Carla, a seventeen-year-old beauty dying of a brain tumor.

"We want her to have some semblance of a normal life for as long as she can," Carla's mother said. Already I saw in her eyes that expression I had come to recognize. She had mentally experienced her lovely daughter's death over and over again, perhaps in some self-protective attempt at preparation. I knew, however, that there was no such thing as being prepared. The expression in her eyes might be premature, but I also knew that it would never go away.

I didn't tell Dottie about my new assignment. I talked about the boy who had infectious mononucleosis, or the girl with the strep throat, but somehow Dottie found out about Carla and gave me her usual maternal tongue-lashing. Dottie would always be my adopted Jewish mother!

"What are you, some kind of masochist?" her lecture began. I told her that I was, of course.

"What kind of perverse kicks do you get out of putting yourself through this?" she demanded.

"I've had enough of this, Dot. If you care about me and really think you know me, you also know that I *do* get something out of working where I feel I'm needed, where I can help."

"Honey, you know I love ya', but this must be tough on you, and who needs all of it?"

"Maybe *I* need to be there because I also lost a child, and by comforting Carla's mother, I am making some kind of sense out of it all."

"Okay, I'll shut up. It's a deal. You know what you're doing, I hope."

Larry had overheard part of our conversation.

"How do you feel about Janni working with terminally ill students?" Dottie asked him conspiratorially.

He shrugged. "As long as it doesn't really get her down, and she wants to do it," he said amiably.

"It's *bound* to get her down, Larry," Dottie argued.

"I think she'll be the best one to decide that," he said. "Now that I'm making a career change and am back in college myself, we're having trouble coordinating our schedules. Scheduling home students is much easier than the inflexibility of working part time at the hospital.''

''Yes, but I'm talking about the kind of students she takes on, not the job itself,'' Dottie said.

''Well,'' Larry replied, ''Jann doesn't hassle me when I have to stay up all hours working on a book-illustrating job, or when I can't get away for a weekend. I just trust her judgment. That's all. We do what we have to do.''

One afternoon when I arrived at Carla's home, I found her mother as ashen pale as her daughter. She took me aside in the kitchen before I went in to Carla.

''Jann, I'm having a rough time,'' she said falteringly. ''I've been doing so well, until—''

''Carla wants to talk about dying?'' I asked her directly, guessing.

''Yes.''

''And?''

''I just can't talk about it. Maybe it's superstition, but . . . to talk about it is to . . . accept it.''

''Perhaps it's *time* to accept it?'' I felt as if I were groping in a dark room, trying to feel my way through this with her.

''Time? But to accept it means to let go, and I'm not ready for that.''

''Do you think that Carla's let go?'' I felt my heart pound at my own question, long-ago recollections making my chest ache.

''Yes,'' she said at last. ''Just this past week I can see a change in her. I tell her it's morose, but that's cruel. She really wants to discuss it, and''—she covered her face with both hands—''I just can't.''

The tears came in heaving sobs, and we held each other

until the impatient whistling of the tea kettle on the stove made Carla call out.

"Mother, can you hear that?" For a moment, neither of us could.

Carla wore the look of death that day. She spoke slowly, as if to savor each word and my response. Her movements were slow and deliberate, and as she lifted a book on the table beside her bed the effort and fatigue it caused were evident.

"I have a special request of you today," she said softly. I pulled my chair closer, since her voice kept fading away until it was barely audible. "When you love someone, you owe them the truth," she said. "You also owe them permission to be honest with you, too."

I half guessed what was coming and clenched my teeth with nervousness, wondering how I would handle it.

"Please tell my mother that I'm not going to lick this cancer thing after all. Please tell her that I need to talk about it—with *her!*"

"You're a very wise girl," I said, fighting back the tears. "You know how she feels, don't you?"

Carla nodded, eyes downcast. "This is so hard on her," she said in that breathless little voice. "I want her to understand so many things."

I later learned that Carla and her mother had a long talk just before the girl's final hospitalization.

Meanwhile, from Vietnam, I learned that Diep's sister Minh, in a much better situation than Diep, now faced her own dilemma, generally because her beloved son was an outcast Amerasian. Freddy's intelligence and talents were superior, and Minh grieved that they might be wasted. Opportunities that would eventually fall to Vietnamese children would be denied Freddy as a half-American in that country. Minh had read or been told that the United States was limiting the number of Amerasian children who could come to the States, and her despair was evident. Her letter, which arrived in August, was plaintive.

The American children here, the Communists say, are the end of the bad American regime. "You can see how the Americans think of their children, the real refugees of war who America so soon forgets," they tell us. Please help us, too. We have no other way, no one else to help us get out.

In October of 1983, Diep sent another anguished letter.

My Dearest Sister Jannice,

Almost eight years now I have worked here with my girls on the large plateau and fields. I am so much older than my age. I feel the hopeless of my life now, see the end ahead of me. This is my life. I am agricultural leader with no place to go, no other life but this one in the mud and labor. My heart is so heavy I cannot breathe sometimes. Sister, I know you do all you can, but are helpless too.

With all my heart and loves I want always to thank you for the hope you give me, which is heartfelt in you. God blessed me with you, and never could I find another one such as you, Sister. But, my life is over. I forget everything. Days have no hours. Months have no weeks. One day is another and I see no future. I will die here with many regrets in this life. Almost eight years and I think it could be eighty. My heart is deeply hurt when I look at my girls, now becoming young women with no future. Jeanie is nearly a woman, and Jolie too. They don't have cheery time. They must work just to find the food, and we pray for food daily. I was always slim. Now I am more slim and don't feel well. Soon I will not be useful to anyone.

Someone here say that there is veterans' organization that will help us. You write them? I'll enclose the address my friend give me.

Sister, will you please send us some material in black or brown, tan or dark blue? You can send three yards in one bag and they don't take. You don't send over three yards, or we must pay much tax. Please send in care of Minh, and thank you very much.

Your sister,
Diep

In another letter the following month, Diep told about Jolie having to walk seven miles to school every day, and seven miles home again, before beginning her work in the field. The bicycle had broken down, and someone had stolen it before it could be replaced. "I have seen someone murdered for his bicycle," Diep said.

"School"—students of all ages in one room—consisted of math and economics with an emphasis, of course, on government and politics. The school's maintenance was the responsibility of the students. Students were required to supply all the food for the teachers, too.

Sometimes I had to work hard in the rain. The mud up to my knees, Sister. Eight years and all my life, and no change. Oh, I pray, Sister, that we be blessed some day. I want to let go and cannot. Please write me and tell me about your life in the United States, about Mr. Larry and your children. I want to think about them and you.

Then came the letter saying that Jolie was very sick. Diep's anguish came through, equaled by my own at not being able to help her.

Her next letter also contained some disturbing news.

Dear Sister,

Tomorrow I must leave Ho Chi Minh City and return to Central Highlands area. I write this to let you know that Jolie go with me. We must go by bus the long way, about 650 miles and will take us two days to get there. We need cough syrup. Very expensive over here and we don't have and need it very much. Sister, a friend wrote me about American bone bodies they found and keep. Please be careful when you write me about it, because we keep the secret. If the government knows, they make trouble for us. If you want to know more, please write and ask. Many poor Americans over here who lost their decision to go home. I feel so sad for them. They live like sewer animal. All my loves going to you.

Diep

In an earlier letter, Diep had mentioned that some Montagnard acquaintances had found the remains of three American flyers and had hidden them as future "investments." One of these men became wealthy by selling American bones to a Vietnamese couple, who were to have sold them back to the Communists to use as barter with the Americans. The only hitch was that after the Montagnard had sold his find, the police had questions that he couldn't answer, and he was promptly thrown in prison.

"There are numerous confirmed reports about Americans over there," Dottie's husband, Randy, said when I showed him the letter. He had been an officer until his retirement four years earlier and was still in the army reserve. "That's no big secret, you know. Some guys chose to remain behind with their Vietnamese wives and girl friends. Some stayed with their kids, and some just got stranded. Many, of course, are POWs."

"I've read that the Vietnamese people are required to notify their government immediately when they find Americans in hiding, or even their bodies. Gruesome as it sounds, Americans living or dead are like money in the bank. Diep might be using information about those bodies to try bartering with our government," Dottie suggested.

"Well, if she is, that's a courageous and dangerous game," Randy replied. "The Communists take a pretty dim view of people concealing that kind of information."

Diep had made it clear that she took issue with such practices, and in her next letter to me she indicated that she simply wanted to contact the proper authorities so that the men's families could know of their fate.

Dearest Sister,

An old friend tell me as a favor about three American bone bodies he find in forest. He tell me that plane go down behind his home and the pilot and two Marines die in wreckage. I have their names, birthdates and religions from their tags and give to you so maybe their families know they die in Vietnam and find the peace. I could get in bad trouble, Sister, so please do not write me about them again but only find their families and let them know. Again, this information could mean bad trouble for me. . . .

Love,
Diep
November 13, 1983

I went to work on this immediately.

It was then I realized that this was going to be another difficult assignment.

In mid-January of 1984, Diep wrote with hopeful news.

Dearest Sister,

I learn today that the government will allow Amerasian children leave country, but the mothers must stay behind. They say it is the law that mothers cannot go too, and only the children go. My sister Minh cry very hard, and she ask how can the United States government be so cruel to separate mothers from their children. Then I say that it is not just the United States that make that ruling, and that if our children are safe and have opportunity that is the most important thing of all. Minh agrees with that.

Perhaps I shall let Jeanie go if she wants to go, but keep Jolie here with me. Jolie say she cannot leave her mother, and I do not think I could bear to have both my children leave me forever. I know in my heart that I would never see them again, and go to my grave with only their memory before my eyes.

Dear Sister, I do not know what to do. If my girls come to you and you adopt them, I can die in peace knowing that. Maybe you send their pictures to me often, to ease my aching heart some. . . .

Diep

Dear Diep,

Of course I will take your children if they come, and will do everything I can to bring you here to join them. Please don't give up. Please remember that I'm here to help in any way that I can.

On February 3, 1984, she replied.

My Dear Sister,

Your letter come to me here, and my heart is heavy with tears. My girls have no future in this country, which is so poor and torn apart from the war. They are the brown-haired children who are rejected and all things will be denied to them. No education. No position in life. But they do not want to leave me here and come to the United States, and I cannot come. I will watch them work until their death, growing into young women and old ones because of their hard work, and I brought them into this life for this sadness.

Diep

Dearest Sister Diep,

My children are grown up now, and when I look at the photographs of Jeanie and Jolie when they were little children, it is so hard to believe that you and I have corresponded nearly all of our children's lives! How much has happened to us, Diep, and what is more remarkable, how we have held unto the faith—you and I— that someday we might meet each other in a happy time. Please don't give up now. Sometimes I worry about that. I will continue to write to whomever I can to find some way to get you out of Vietnam *with* your daughters. I will never give up, and you must never give up either! I am sending you some aspirin and vitamins in care of your sister. Some candy will come for the girls and Freddy.

Love,
Jann

(Apparently this letter, sent in March of 1984, was never received, nor were the candy, vitamins, or aspirin.)

* * *

Shortly thereafter, a letter came from Diep's sister Minh. In it she told how tired Diep had appeared to her the last time she had seen her and how thin Jolie was. A letter had come two days earlier from her son, Freddy, requesting vitamins for Jolie and saying that they were worried about her. The sadness and resignation in their letters depressed me, and Larry was also subdued as he read each letter over and over.

Finally he said, "Dottie is right, you know. You've invested too much emotional energy in this thing, over too long an expanse of time. I suspect that the most dangerous period is over for them, and by now the new government has also settled down. Surely after all this time, Diep and the girls have become adjusted to their lives."

"They really don't complain," I replied, "but what I have read and heard tells me that their lives are very hard."

"Well," he said, "if every time you receive a letter from Vietnam you're going to be sad and depressed, I'd say that it isn't very good for you. Better just make up your mind that you've done all you can do from this end, and be done with it."

There was wisdom in his words; I had to acknowledge that as I wrapped a box of yarn and new knitting needles for Diep and prepared it for mailing.

A few weeks later, Larry handed me a letter from Minh, as we were hurrying to get ready to meet friends for dinner at a restaurant. I put the letter on my dresser and forgot it in the dash to be on time.

The following morning I noticed the unopened letter and tore it open with my usual nervous anticipation. With the utmost simplicity, the letter from Minh broke the news that

*. . . my sister, she get out of Vietnam with her daughters
and go to the Philippines on November 30, 1984.*

I held the letter for the longest time, not believing the words, expecting that I had read them too quickly and had misunderstood their meaning. I stared at the letter in my hands, almost expecting it to self-destruct or disappear at any moment. Then I showed it to Larry, and he and I stared at each other, speechless, barely able to take in its significance. In Minh's simple words was the culmination of over eighteen years of dreams and prayers and pain . . . and hope.

The joy of that moment was counterbalanced the following week when I was asked to tutor another student dying with a malignant brain tumor. Her name was Arka, and she was seventeen years old. Our first meeting was brief but not sad.

I went to her high school to pick up her books and assignments, met with her counselor there, and paid a short visit to her math teacher.

"She's an excellent student," he said solemnly. "When we heard the prognosis, it never occurred to any of us that she'd still want to finish her work. I guess . . ." He gazed out the window as if forgetting momentarily that I was there. "I guess that by doing familiar tasks, like homework, it's a way of denying that you're going to die."

"From what I hear, Arka doesn't deny her dying at all," I told him. "To the contrary, she passed through that stage months ago."

"Then why on earth . . ." he began, distress in his face.

"When I was a teenager I was told about St. Francis of

Assisi playing chess with a fellow monk. When the other monk asked him, 'If you had only until sunset this day to live, how would you spend your last hours?' St. Francis is said to have replied, 'I would continue to play chess.' ''

"I don't get it," the math teacher said as he folded several homework sheets between the pages of a textbook.

"Never mind." I reached for the homework and book. "But I think Arka has come to terms with her illness better than anyone else."

As I drove to her home near the foothills of Mt. Diablo, familiar landmarks slid by me with a rhythm of their own. I passed the green Contra Costa hills, spring-decorated with orange poppies, dark blue lupine, and yellow mustard; the mountain loomed ahead, the majestic overseer for the valley below, as the dark cloud shadows of a rainstorm moved across its slopes.

I parked in the driveway of Arka's house, turned off the ignition, and enjoyed a moment in silence. Yellow and pink roses lined the driveway, explosions of pastel color and fragrance that Arka would not enjoy another year. That realization struck an emotional blow, although its significance did not fully register.

"She's waiting in her bedroom for you," her mother said in hushed tones as I passed through the door. "Arka really likes you. I'm so glad the district picked you." She paid the compliment with a warm, sincere smile and took my hand. "When I spoke with the director at the district office, he told me you've had other students with Arka's . . . condition." She paused and I tried to figure out what she really wanted to know.

"Do your students talk about how . . . they . . . they . . ."

"Sometimes they find it easier to talk about their concerns with a person outside the family," I told her.

"Do they always face it head-on the way Arka does?"

"No," I replied. "Sometimes kids want to protect their family, so they continue to pretend that they'll get better and return to school. Arka's pretty up front about things, isn't she?"

Her mother nodded.

"And you're afraid that she's given up, when perhaps she shouldn't?" I guessed. The woman's eyes filled with tears, and she turned her face away.

"I'm afraid that maybe she doesn't *want* to live!"

"Oh, she doesn't impress me that way at all," I said gently. "She's just accepting this thing, and according to what I've been told, her doctors offer no encouragement that it's reversible or that there will be any remission at this point. Isn't that right?"

"But we've always believed that as long as you . . . fight . . ."

"There comes a point, I think, when one has to turn to concerns other than fighting for life," I said. "Maybe she instinctively knows that now is the time for other . . ."

"Business? That's what she calls it, *business.*"

"Yes, I suppose that's a good word for it," I said, taking her hand. "I wish I could be more comforting for you. I lost a child of my own not too many years ago, and we were unable to have the talks that you and your own daughter can have. You are both in a position to comfort each other, you know."

The welling tears spilled down her cheeks. "And I have another friend to talk to as well," she said, squeezing my hand.

"I'm here for you both, if it helps," I reassured her.

Chapter Nine

New Beginnings

Diep's first letter from the Philippines was filled with elation.

> Dear Sister,
>   It is so hard to believe! We arrived in Philippines' Orientation Camp by way of Thailand and Hong Kong. We cannot come to you direct, and will stay here six months and learn the American way of life. We see the movie here *Moscow on the Hudson* three times. It shown to us to help us understand the problems of the refugee in America, but it really very funny!

The idea of a Robin Williams movie being presented as instruction for refugees, many of whom couldn't even speak English, was hilarious in itself.

Diep wrote that she and her girls were attending daily classes designed to help with their adjustment once they

arrived in the States. She said that another six months'
wait was frustrating, but in light of the years they had
waited so far, they could face that. "This will make it
easier for you too, Sister, since we will be coming to you
more self-sufficient."

Mrs. Waltermire's contacts with the Refugee Resettlement offices in New York made arrangements for a cospon-
sorship with St. Andrew's Presbyterian Church, located
in the city where we live, and they had contacted me immediately when the news came about Diep's release from
Vietnam. A manual arrived from this agency, accompanied by forms asking for information about Diep, Jeanie,
and Jolie. The manual's purpose was to provide information for the sponsor, and it spelled out responsibilities.

There were questionnaires pertaining to each of the
Nguyens and their health and ability to cope. There was
some information for me regarding their school program
in the Philippines and some basic information about their
own culture.

Thus it became immediately apparent that this organization was behind us to assist and to watch out for the
refugees they had helped sponsor. St. Andrew's Church,
its minister, the Reverend Robert Bennett, and the World
Outreach Chairman, Mrs. Adelaid Chavez, contacted us
and inquired about Diep's plans and needs; they made me
aware of the genuine excitement among the church congregation over her pending arrival.

"I received a phone call this morning from one of the
parishioners," I told Larry the day after Minh's letter arrived, "and already people are offering furniture and
clothes for our new little family." We were overwhelmed
when an excellent TV set was donated by a lady whose
husband had promised to buy her a new one. Couches,

chairs, tables, beds, and linens were quickly tagged and stored for Diep and her girls.

As soon as the word was out in St. Andrew's, friendly and compassionate people began to set aside everything they could think of that one day soon would help give Diep a new start in her life. "When she finally has her own apartment," Larry said, "she'll be set. They are really helping her begin her life in this country. The word 'Welcome' seems to be printed on every item that has been donated so far."

People came forward with dishes, towels, silverware, glasses, and plates. Many individuals kept useful items in their own homes after letting me know they were there when Diep was ready for them. Mrs. Chavez volunteered to drive Diep and the girls to appointments when we were unable to do so, and other church members also offered transportation whenever it was needed.

"You're under no obligation to join or attend the church," Mr. Bennett said one day. "Of course, we want to have you very much, but there is absolutely no obligation here at all." I guess that I'd know that, but I deeply appreciated hearing him say it. And, naturally, I had every intention of meeting with the congregation of St. Andrew's with Diep and Jeanie and Jolie after their arrival, since I felt having the members of that church get to know the people they had helped so much and were cosponsoring was important.

The warmth, support, and kind assistance from people who had never known any of us prior to their agreement to help sponsor the Nguyens impressed me greatly, especially after I learned just what sponsorship really entailed. Visits to doctors, to and from the County Health Department, to the Department of Motor Vehicles, to the Social

Security offices, to the County Health Care Services at the hospital, as well as many other essential appointments would have to be made.

I was suddenly aware that the responsibility of taking in a family from such an entirely different culture was not just a simple matter of giving them Western clothes and food, not that I had been quite so naive as to think that. A kind Vietnamese lady who worked for Social Services in the area pointed out that we would be contending with many emotional adjustments that might be terribly rough at first—not just for Diep, but for us as well.

"Homesickness is a real sickness," she said. "Most people coming from Vietnam are convinced that they'll never again see those loved ones they left behind. Everything is so different, so strange here; even the rapid pace of our daily living is scary for them. Modern conveniences that we take for granted can be intimidating for some Vietnamese refugees, and of course there is always the language barrier."

I thought I knew all of this, but suddenly I realized what an awesome task this could be, and I hoped that our mutual caring and compassion would carry us through. I guess that I never *really* understood what a "culture shock" it would be for Diep. In my anxiety over her safety and getting her out of Vietnam, the multitude of other potential problems had been the least of my concerns.

"You know," Mrs. Waltermire told me on the phone, "Diep could have come to you directly, but she *chose* to go to the camp in the Philippines. She wisely thought it would make her own adjustments and your life, too, much easier if she did."

That idea astounded me. After all these years, I would have expected that she wouldn't have had such patience!

She and her girls were having a six-month course in how to be an American, not only to assist them in their adjustments, but to help us, too! Their first Christmas away from home, in 1984, was apparently very sad.

Dear Sister,

I shall send you Christmas pictures of us here. My girls attend the English classes and learn very much. We are well and doing o.k. We have the tape you send us with music "Memories" on it and love it very much. You tape your voice, and it is soft and beautiful for us. . . .

Love,
Diep

January 5, 1985

Dear Diep,

I still cannot believe you are really out of Vietnam. How did you manage it? It came as such a wonderful surprise, but I am also in shock. I had all but given up! Sometimes I think about you and the girls in the refugee camp in the Philippines, and just don't believe it has finally happened.

Love,
Jann

My Dear Sister,

When we meet, I will tell you all about it. I was not valuable to them anymore, as I am getting older and my girls are the half-Americans. There is more, but we will talk when first we meet.

We miss our homeland, the poor little country torn apart by the war. We will always think about South Vietnam with tears, but now we are safe, and the first part of my dream has come true.

How we long for the day when we see each other for the first time, after all these years!

> Love,
> Diep

Dear Sister Diep,

The letter arrived today from New York's offices of the Refugee Resettlement Program that you and your children will be leaving the Philippines mid-May, 1985. They say that we will have the exact date of your arrival in the San Francisco airport one week in advance. I am so excited.

> Jann

Dearest Sister,

It is coming so close. I am confused and afraid. All these years I have dreamed and prayed for the moment, and now that it is nearly here . . . .

> Love,
> Diep

During the months when Diep was in the refugee camp (they called it "Ho-Chi-Minhville" in the Philippines), I decided to collect all of her letters and the copies of my own and write this book. I sent her a letter outlining my intentions.

She did not respond right away. I then wrote two articles as the basis for the book I planned to write. The *San Francisco Chronicle* published the first of those articles just a week prior to Diep's planned arrival, and a local television reporter contacted me for an interview. His intention was to film the actual arrival of Diep and Jeanie and Jolie at the airport.

How many times in the months ahead would I look at

their taped arrival and see the usually stoic Jeanie burst into tears at our first meeting in the airport. At the time I could not know that the family's one fear was that I would have a change of heart at the last minute and not be there. Only months later would I fully understand how frightened they were, and why. From this I learned that we may think we understand a situation, but that our very confidence can block out the real picture.

Jeanie gave this poignant account of leaving Vietnam:

"What will happen to me in the new life? I asked myself this question when I approached the San Francisco airport. Often have I heard it said that life is not easy with the Americans, and that America really is not Heaven. I could not speak English to you well when we first meet, and my sister and I were afraid to open our mouth and say anything wrong.

"Would you be disappointed to meet us? I did not know how to express my deepest thoughts. But I believed in you who was our sponsor, and who had been my mother's friend. I knew you would help us Vietnamese refugees without our country in this new life.

"You appeared to us that first second with real emotion and warmness and affection, as my mother said you were sweet and kind. How wonderful you are, I thought! I had wished in the plane that time would fly slowly so I could compose my mind. After we meet you, I had no worries anymore. Your smile made me know we were okay. We will never forget.

"This is my saddest memory: After I filled in the papers for the authority people to allow my mother and sister and me out of the country, telling them my mother could not read or write without help, that she was not too bright, they posted our names on the List for Departure for November 29, 1984, but told us that when we leave Vietnam, we never see our home or family again for all our lives.

"It was our final decision, to leave or to stay. 'You will look back at your country for the last time,' we were told, 'and it will be only in your memory from the minute you step through the Tan Son Nhut airport doors.'

"There were crowds and crowds of people who were friends and relatives of the Departing Persons. At 9:00 A.M., the Departing Persons had to go into a separation room to comply with all the necessary formalities before leaving Saigon, Vietnam. At that time, everyone burst out crying in the separation room. It was made of glass and wood, and through the windows you could see all of your friends and family for the last time. After that, you might get glimpse of them from airport as you waited for plane to board, but you knew that you would never speak to them or touch them ever again. That was the order of the Communist police.

"They were afraid that we would take money or gold or records with us when we left Vietnam, so we and our belongings were checked carefully. I remember the last time I hugged my aunts and other friends and family members in my arms, hands in hands, eyes in eyes. . . . We stood so still before saying Good-Bye.

"Oh, how I have loved my country, Vietnam, where I was born, but now I must leave it and find the new life. And when the airplane flew up into the immense sky, I felt such hurt inside. It was the most expensive cost of my life, and for any Vietnamese refugee wanting to escape, to give up one's home."

Jolie recounted her relief on their arrival: "A Vietnamese lady at the airport who worked there came on the plane and said to my mother: 'Mrs. Jansen is here and waits for you.' Then I knew you didn't give us up, and I felt so happy that we have the love from you, an American; God had blessed us at last.

Jolie described what their first few days in America were like.

"When my mother was ill after we arrived in your home, you took care of her with all your heart. Everything we see was strange. First time, we did not know how to buy anything at store, what money to use or how much, how to call on the telephone or use any machines in the house. I felt so confused, because I had never seen anything like these in my life before. I knew then how hard it would be to learn so much.

"I remember when we meet someone new, and you introduced us. You said: 'I have a new family.' How lovely were those spoken words. I did not feel lonely anymore. Before, in my country, Americans were shunned after 1975 when I was only eight. I was afraid that Americans would shun me, too, because I was also half-Vietnamese. Now I knew that I had had wrong thinking.

"I often think about my family living in Ban Me Thout when we were so poor. No more house, no food, and my mother had just a little money with two white hands to live and work in that hard land. The famine threatened us and how hungry I was.

"I would eat anything, then. I ate the bud of the banana tree, the leaves of the red pepper tree, and some kinds of weeds that live in the fields. We never had meat or fish. We tried to get over this until the ripening of the rice. I don't want to remember how my poor mother worked so hard, was so tired when she fell asleep at night, but I cannot forget."

Jeanie gave her first impressions of life in the States, too.

"In the car after you meet us, I thought how beautiful

America was. I saw so many cars in the garage at airport and thought I was living in a dream. There were so many things to see, all new and wonderful, and most of all I knew you had a free country. No one would stop us on the way to your home and question us or hurt us. I thought that my new life would start with my mind and my hands, and I would live in freedom forever.

"In your house was a piano and guitar, and your house was quiet and nice. There was the pond with big fish, like a lake, and I knew you loved animals. It was all so wonderful for me. I was so surprised that Americans planted just the grass in their yards and wanted just the grass. The house so big and beautiful! My eyes and heart were full of wonder at so much. . . ."

Jolie told me later:

"I will never forget the frights I had as a little girl, how I would hug my mother tightly and close my eyes when the firebombs came. Sometimes I prayed 'til dawn, but even when the guns stopped my frights still stayed in my mind. I will never forget when we ran home that April day in 1975 and everyone was running in all directions, and my mother said to me: 'Run quickly and don't look closely at anything.' I saw one dead woman who was pregnant and had just died. She lay down full length on the street, and I nearly ran into her.

"When we went to Central Highlands, the peace replaced the war, but the hunger replaced the firebombs. I now feared as much to die by the hunger as I had feared to die by the bombs. The peace with its hunger made me an animal, starving and poor.

"I felt bitter toward my father who had gone away. My cousin Freddy felt bitter, too. I have never had a father to call 'Daddy' and have never seen his face. That was unhappy for me. I could not understand what my American father think, why he not write me a letter to wonder about me or care about my life. Did he wonder ever if I was alive or dead? He had gone to America, leaving me in Vietnam, bequeathing me the brown hair and eyes and white skin, and he never knew what would become of me. What would he say when Vietnamese children mocked me and turned on me?

"What did my father do for me? He made me, but it was nothing to him. He left me only the tears. I would think: 'If I had a good father who loved me, he would make my life different. I would be happy now, and if he had not abandoned me, I would not be so miserable as this.' I wanted so to write to him but did not know how to find him. Yes, I thought, he has forgotten me, but I keep his photograph and the necklace he gave me when I was two years old. It was the forbidden picture of an American soldier, but my mother had saved it and given it to me. I would never lose it or throw it away. It was all I knew of my father. . . ."

It was Jolie who apparently had the most pain over not having a father. Jeanie told me, "I never think about my father. I have no feeling at all about him, no feeling," but then she burst into tears. Jolie's reaction was different, however. An expression of longing would come over her face whenever the subject came up. One evening she, Jeanie, their mother, and I went to the local library to look through the collection of phone directories there. Thinking that I was helping them, I wanted to locate the man who had fathered Jolie, so that she could write to him and tell him that she was safe in America. Diep assured me that they wanted nothing from him, only to let him know that they were here.

"He is a good man," she said. "If he wants to help Jolie in any way, it will be left up to him. If not, that is okay, too."

We were unsuccessful in finding his name listed in the last town where Diep remembered he had lived, and so I forgot about it for a time. Then one evening my daughter Donice phoned me: "Mother, I have his address and phone number." With the help of a military friend she had located Jolie's father, who was retired by now.

"I'd better think this one over before contacting him," I told her. "He's probably happily married, and perhaps his wife doesn't even know he had a child in Vietnam."

In the meantime, adjustments to all of the new experiences were quickly made. All of us had many laughs over the weeks that Diep and her girls lived with us. One evening while Larry and I were out, the girls decided to help us by planting a vegetable garden. They were perplexed by all of the grass growing in the yard and promptly began to hoe up a section of it. "Crazy Americans," they thought, "planting just grass!"

When they had first arrived, I thought that a nice warm bubble bath would be pure luxury for them. I began to draw the bath water and filled it with bubble bath, leaving the box in the bathroom. *No one* would venture into that tub that first night because they were puzzled and perhaps a little afraid of the bubbles. They just couldn't understand, but a few days later one of my pet dogs walked into the house smelling wonderful. It turned out that the girls had rubbed dry bubble bath into the dog's fur.

Jeanie, who was mechanically inclined, was particularly fascinated with the lawn mower. Inventive by nature as well, when something broke down, she had the ability to improvise a repair. Jolie, on the other hand, turned dewy eyed whenever anything came on television depicting an infant, even the diaper commercials.

They enjoyed all television at any time of the day, but David Carradine's "Kung Fu" series was their favorite.

Diep was delighted to be able to have all of the yarn she could imagine, and she immediately began knitting us sweaters. The fact that the hottest part of the year was fast approaching did not daunt her! Her handmade sweaters were gorgeous—made, of course, without any written patterns—and they fit perfectly. She could do anything from cable knit to the fancy stitches that she studied and copied from sweaters in the stores.

Larry and I had never eaten soup for breakfast in our lives, yet from the first morning that Diep and the girls arrived, we were treated to their soups.

I would get up and go into the kitchen early in the morning to discover that my little family had already had their noodle soup for breakfast, and that they had left some for Larry and me. The aroma of noodle soup was now one of the first smells of the day, and breakfast soup just one of the new habits I would acquire.

My cooking has never earned raves from my family, but it was definitely not to the Nguyens' liking at first. They ate very little, in fact, until they felt more comfortable around the kitchen and we began purchasing foods they recognized and liked. They discovered the dried Chinese soups that sell inexpensively in the supermarkets, and Jeanie became quickly addicted to "just soup, thank you!"

I'll never forget the first "treat" we planned—taking them to a Vietnamese restaurant. The hostess, delighted that her new guests were Vietnamese and so recently from Vietnam, brought out dish after dish of food. Diep was stunned at the quantity, and after eating just a small bit, she stopped and became quite upset. Later she explained, "In Vietnam, we worked very hard for the food, and here there was so much—*too* much for me—that I saw all of that food, and cry." She thought about her friends still in the Central Highlands, especially those who might starve the first year a crop was planted, or those who would go hungry if their crops failed. When she thought about her younger sisters and brothers, family members who were still struggling to survive, the quantity of food in that restaurant made her angry. "We did not need," she explained, "and it seemed a waste."

Our good intentions and those of the restaurant owner failed miserably, but that was before Larry and I fully understood. It was when Diep gave me more details than the many letters she had sent from the Central Highlands had contained that I comprehended that they had indeed been on the brink of starvation more than once.

I also learned that the main reason she was released from Vietnam was that her children were Amerasian, although having a place to go when she arrived in the United States also made a big difference. By signing a promissory note with the International Governmental Commission for Migration, a voluntary agency based in Geneva, Diep had been granted a no-interest loan. It was a revolving fund, so that as she paid it back, the monies would go toward assisting other refugees. Without that loan, she could not have afforded to come to the United States.

Without the intervention and assistance of the Church World Services Organization, contacted repeatedly by Mrs. Waltermire who had been recommended by George Miller's assistant, she could easily still be in Vietnam today, working in the rice fields.

"There are just two things I don't like," Larry said one evening when Diep insisted on fixing supper, "horseradish and cilantro!" He carefully picked out the green cilantro leaves from his soup and placed them on the saucer while Diep and Jolie laughed. In Vietnam, cilantro is a commonly used herb. Diep had been excited at each vegetable she recognized the first time we took her to the grocery store.

Although I had been empathic about them feeling free to use the kitchen and help themselves to whatever they wanted to eat at any time, every once in a while something I did would startle them and they could retreat like frightened quail. Their appreciation was always obvious, however, and the security at having their own room was also obvious. Whenever I had occasion to go to their room, it seemed a well-loved place as if it offered them a special kind of protection and comfort. It was here that they spent much of their time the first few weeks, happy in their own company with their color TV and English/Vietnamese dictionary.

The need to help me or Larry, to become contributing members of our family, was paramount for them. Although not expressed verbally, Diep's sincere desire to give to us and not be a burden was evident. She ruled her daughters with a strong maternal hand and often used that agricultural leader tone of voice that made her highly respected in the New Economic Zone of Vietnam. Her girls—always immediately obedient—seemed to know that tone of voice quite well.

I was fascinated with their mutual appreciation for each other, their knowledge of each other. The girls often disagreed and even had their noisy arguments in Vietnamese, which amused us greatly. Somehow, hearing someone quarrel in another language never seems quite so serious as when the quarrel is in your own tongue. But when they teased each other or displayed their quick sense of humor, it was even more delightful.

The two girls had not really used English after the fall of Saigon. Jolie gradually became braver about speaking it. None of them seemed particularly frustrated when we did not understand, and they drew sketches or developed a pantomine whenever necessary. They were wonderful artists.

"For people who haven't used their English in over ten years, they are learning very quickly," Dottie pointed out. The rapidity with which they were now learning astounded me, too, and I wondered how I would have fared if I had been suddenly set down in the middle of South Vietnam on my own.

After meals the girls always quickly cleared the table and began to wash the dishes and clean up the kitchen. If I started to do this, Diep made it clear that this was their task, not mine. She wouldn't allow me to play hostess, and that was final.

Dottie and I met for lunch at a local restaurant one day to discuss her troubles. She had been having a rough time recently. Shortly after her reconciliation with Randy, his daughter had come to live with them, and she wasn't easy.

"Cindy's pitting Randy and his exwife against each other, and I think he's gonna be the loser," Dottie said, lighting her cigarette. She was oblivious to the one still burning in the ashtray in front of her.

"How old is his stepdaughter?"

"Sixteen, I think sixteen," Dottie said. "I walk around the house on tiptoe to avoid her. She hates my guts."

"Are you sure about that?"

"Yeah, no doubt about it."

"How come she's living with you, anyhow?"

" 'Cause Randy was the only person who ever showed her kindness in her life, and her mom's got a new and unstable relationship now."

"What're you going to do, Dottie?"

"Make the best of it, I s'pose," she said, inhaling

deeply and closing her eyes. "This kid has never pulled in a grade higher than a 'C' in her life. She's never washed a dish without complaining, never hosed down a car or pulled a weed. She picks out her clothes by checking the label and price tags first. If they aren't designer rags, or cost a month's paycheck—in this case, Randy's—she's not interested."

"Here, have my ice water and cool off," I kidded.

"No foolin', Janni, this kid and I just don't understand each other." Dottie shook her head more in sadness than anger. "She said she might want to be a nurse someday. So I tried to get her interested in the Candy Striper program at the hospital, working as a volunteer. Well, she'd have none of that volunteer-without-pay stuff."

"She's old enough to get a job?"

"Yeah—oh, I don't know. Randy's so damned protective. I think the truth of it is he doesn't want his ex to think he can't afford to support this kid."

"What are her interests, then?" I asked.

"Beats me. I think her chief interest is a four-letter word in the plural, *boys!* Yeah, that's Number One Interest these days."

"That's pretty normal, I'd say."

"Maybe, but it's pretty useless if that's all she's interested in, don't you think?"

"Marry her off and your problems are over." I tried levity again.

"I wouldn't wish that narcissistic little vamp on any guy, and that's the truth," Dottie said bitterly. "Trouble is, Randy's so carried away with this father thing, and—God!" She looked up and seemed to pale. In the doorway of the restaurant stood a young woman looking around as if searching for someone. Dottie appeared confused, torn between wanting to hide behind me and waving at the girl.

"What is it, Dottie?"

"Shhhhh."

"I don't—"

"Jeeez!—It's Cindy. She's coming over. She's spotted us!"

An attractive young blonde walked up to our table and, with self-assured poise, patted Dottie on the head as she sat down with us. Enormous earrings, like gaudy saucers, hung from her ears, and her dry, teased hair was spiked in a blond halo around her rather small face. Cindy was certainly attractive, but she worked hard to conceal it.

"Your note said you were here, Dottie, and since I needed some cash *badly,* I thought I'd track you down."

"How come you're not in school?" Dottie asked in a dutiful tone of voice.

"B-o-r-i-n-g, really *boring,*" the girl replied grimacing.

"You hungry?" Dottie asked in that same dutiful voice, and I realized that she was hoping the girl would say "No."

"Yeah, come to think of it. Where's a menu?" She pulled one from a neighboring table that was not occupied.

Obviously nervous about this intrusion, Dottie tried to make conversation. "Jann's got a Vietnamese family living with her. They've only been in this country a few weeks."

"Yeah? Great." Cindy's lack of interest couldn't have been clearer. "Does salad come with the fried prawns?" she asked the waitress who had appeared to take her order.

Dottie tried again. "The woman and her girls survived the war, and . . ."

"Are they still fighting over there?" Cindy asked Dottie, but judging by her immediate distraction as two young men sat down at the next table, she was not interested in the answer.

The rest of the meal was eaten in relative silence. Dottie insisted on picking up the tab, and as we turned to leave I realized that Cindy was already standing at the men's table and waving us off.

"Jeez," Dottie said. "I just realized that I never introduced you two."

"No loss." I smiled as I patted her arm.

When I arrived home, Jolie and Jeanie were washing our two Dobermans. I stood in the patio doorway watching as the girls poured water over the sudsy dogs, who were tied by the their leashes to a stake. The dogs endured it and the girls enjoyed it, and the giggles and happiness of that scene will remain with me always. The contrast between this moment and the scene in the restaurant with a highly privileged and spoiled young girl, who only *appeared* to be older than my Vietnamese girls, was shocking. While I don't like to think that deprivation is necessary to make people stronger and more appreciative, I do question the value of affluence in building character.

I had not attended services since my Marna died, so it felt strange to be sitting in the same church where she had been baptized so many years before. The remarkable thing was that today, seated demurely beside me, was Nguyen Thi Diep and her two grown-up daughters. They were actually here. What a wonder!

I felt chills as the choir of St. Andrew's Church sang an anthem. I was afraid that I would cry. The magic of the moment was overwhelming. The music was so powerful, so beautiful. Diep sat dry-eyed, as did her girls, but I knew they felt the same wonder as I. When the congregation stood—so many, many people!—we stood, too. I could see the tears in Jeanie's eyes now, but she held her head high and the tears did not spill. The girls and their mother could not sing, since they did not know the words, but I was sure they understood the general meaning of it all—music, the universal language!

When the service was over and we all slowly filed out, shaking the Reverend Mr. Bennett's hand as we left the church, the joy at Diep's presence and the warm acceptance of her and her children were evident.

Through it all, Diep remained poised, calm, and never flustered. She was gracious and appreciative, and she took everything in stride, as did the girls. It was I who was on the verge of tears much of the time, amazed that it had all really come true. Is this really happening? I found myself asking that question many times in the months to come.

"Diep and the girls came here with such hope, such belief in themselves and their abilities to do *anything,*" I mentioned to Larry one evening as we got ready for bed.

"I know. They had so much confidence, didn't they?"

"That's the point. It seems to be past tense. I don't feel that they're as confident as they were."

"What makes you say that?" He got into bed beside me and turned off the lamp.

"I don't know, exactly. I guess it's just that they don't seem motivated to leave the house unless we take them somewhere. They aren't too adventurous."

"Well," he said softly, "maybe their sense of adventure has been satisfied for their entire lifetime."

"Oh, you know what I mean. Last week we went for a walk, Diep, the girls, and I. I tied little ribbons on the gates and along the pathway as we went, just in case they ever wanted to take the trails themselves; by following the ribbons they wouldn't get lost."

"Those are public bike and jogging trails," he said. "It's unlikely they'd lose their way on those trails, so close to home."

"Well, I just wanted to reassure them, in case they ever wanted to get out and go for a walk. That was over a week ago, and they've never left the house since."

"Be patient and give them time," Larry advised. "They're just insecure."

I was becoming increasingly worried, however, that they seemed so timid about investigating or exploring just our own community. Larry did not think there was any cause for concern, but as I sat out under our pine trees one afternoon after eating my lunch, I watched a mother robin feeding two fluttering babies on a tree branch and fully understood my own fears. The little birds might have remained in the nest much longer if she had not lured them out, although she was still there for them.

Then I went indoors and realized that Jeanie and Jolie were not there.

"They went for bike ride," Diep said with concern. "They gone long while," she said. I saw the worry in her face. "Perhaps policeman stop them and ask them questions, and they no have enough English to speak?"

"They know the way back here, don't they?" I asked her, sharing her worry for the moment. Then the front door opened, and two jubilant girls bounded into the room, laughing as they each held up a handful of colored ribbons.

"I bought something at store," Jeanie said as she handed the loose change to her mother. She triumphantly produced a bottle of 7-Up from a Safeway paper bag. "And the clerk said, 'Have a nice day.' " She giggled.

"And I said, 'Have a nice day!' " This little triumph amused her greatly, and she and Jolie and their mother laughed and laughed.

Then Jeanie went into the kitchen to get five glasses. I felt, somehow, that Larry and I were joining in a special toast as she poured her 7-Up.

Larry and I were dismayed to learn from Diep that some teachers in the Philippines had conducted classes designed to coach refugees on how to apply for welfare. Debates were held where refugees argued the merits and/or disadvantages of relying on welfare assistance. Apparently some of the discussions in the camp had become heated. I had already explained the system to Diep in a letter to her in the Philippines, pointing out that she would be sheltered and supported by us until she could become self-sufficient and so would not need to seek welfare for herself and the girls.

After about another month, I realized that something was happening that I could not have anticipated. Diep and the girls were becoming listless; I observed a general malaise, a lethargy taking over. The television was on much of the time, and their afternoon naps became longer and longer. They did not discuss it, but I sensed their boredom and discouragement. I proposed to Larry that we take them to the Employment Development Offices and try to help them find work.

"That's ridiculous," he said. "Their English is still rough, and they'd be lost. Why, even a trip to the store by themselves is scary for them."

"Many people hold entry-level jobs whose English isn't as good as theirs," I argued. "I'm going to take them tomorrow and see what we can find out."

That morning was spent filling out papers and waiting endlessly. Diep and the girls were understandably nervous, but I sensed that they were excited, too. The job counselors gave them referrals, and off we went to keep three job interviews.

Jeanie and Jolie wore new summer dresses, which I had purchased for this event. They looked beautiful and radiant, and I was optimistic that they would come home successful and inspired.

I'll not soon forget Jeanie walking across the parking lot to the convalescent hospital where she was to be interviewed that day. She did not look back at the car, and I kept wondering if I should accompany her. I decided against it, since it seemed that if she needed a "translator" to help her with the job application and interview, her chances of being hired might be slim.

I had a sinking feeling in my stomach when Jolie, who had applied at another nearby convalescent hospital, came out of her interview, saddened and discouraged. A phone call to the supervisor, requesting information regarding her interview, disclosed that Jolie "had been too frightened to talk." My guess was that she was really having trouble understanding the woman's English, which was overlaid with a strong Spanish accent.

Jeanie, on the other hand, emerged from her interview overjoyed. She had been hired at the minimum wage, which seemed like a fortune to her, and would start the following week.

Diep was promptly hired at MacDonald's part time, and within two weeks Jolie was working at yet another hospital. The family had also been asked to house-sit for a couple from church who would be out of state for three months. Caretaking the church family's home for three months would provide an ideal transition between our home and the one they would eventually rent themselves. And the fact that Jolie's employment and her mother's were within three miles of their new temporary home made the move ideal.

Those times when Larry and I had to work and the Nguyens needed transportation, willing church members were always there to help. However, bicycles donated by the church became the Nguyens' prized possessions, and soon all three of them were bicycling to and from work each day.

Jeanie's employment was nearly eight miles from the house where she and her mother and sister were staying, which meant that she had about a sixteen-mile round trip daily on her bicycle. Working in the convalescent hospital was strenuous, and she was exhausted by the time she got home in the evening.

Within no time she had applied for a position working in the same hospital where Jolie worked, and she was quickly hired. Her ingenuity and independence delighted us, and Larry and I felt that our extended family was truly "on its way" after only two months' time.

I'll never forget that first evening when we left them at the house they were to take care of for three months. The house was small but comfortable, with a pleasant vegetable garden and several fruit trees. I saw Diep's excitement, then watched her vacillate between happiness and homesickness for her "first home in America." We all knew this was a transition stage, yet I could tell that Diep and the girls felt cut off, perhaps abandoned, as we prepared to return to our home, leaving them behind. It was only eight miles to our home, but it could have been eight hundred miles as far as they were concerned. None of the Nguyens cried as we got into our car, but I saw that tears were near the surface.

"We be okay." Diep nodded, smiling as she stood beside the car. The sadness was there in spite of her reassurances.

The minute I arrived home (ten minutes later), I phoned them. They each took turns talking on the telephone, laughing with delight to hear my voice so soon.

For at least two weeks Larry or I either paid them a visit or phoned, and on Sundays I took the family to church. Although our contacts were regular, especially at first, the actual weaning process had already begun. To say that only Diep and the girls felt sad as we began pulling back and easing them into greater independence would be untruthful. The fact is that both Larry and I experienced a certain sense of loss and sadness, although it was I who had felt the greater need to encourage their move. In Vietnam it is not unusual for large numbers of family members to live under one roof, but unfortunately in our country, the opposite is true. I was anxious that the Nguyens be as self-sufficient as I knew they really wanted to be.

In late September of 1985 I was fortunate to find an ad in the paper for a house rental on the same street where Diep was house-sitting. My hope was to create as few changes and adjustments for them as possible, and an inspection of the rental convinced me that this was "their house." It had a nice yard, was quite spacious, and comfortable and was closer to the stores and their jobs.

The fact that it was right across the street from a cemetery didn't concern Diep at all. It was probably this feature that made the rent reasonable and kept the property available until we could all make up our minds.

"Frankly, I think the view is . . . peaceful," quipped Larry. "Why, we could all have a picnic over there sometime."

"Spirits don't bother me," joked Diep. "Just let them stay over there, that's all."

But the cemetery did cause us some concern late one night. Jolie had permission from her mother to work until midnight, and this necessitated her getting a ride from one of the older female employees at the hospital. It seems that the woman was quite superstitious and refused to bring Jolie to her front door when she discovered that the cemetery was right across the road.

Now all three contributed to the family expenses. They even had a savings account, and it was decided that the first major investment would be a secondhand piano. Another perusal of the classified section turned up a wonderful old spinet, and taking the little family out to see their first piano and seeing their pride as they paid $400 out of their own earnings was another mental photograph I'll always treasure.

Within a year, Jeanie had managed to purchase a used car, and the family replaced their TV set with a new one, had a microwave, a VCR, a stereo, and a puppy. They had all of the trappings of a successful American family, and we kidded them relentlessly each time we paid them a visit.

In the meantime, my daughter had contacted Jolie's father. When he learned that Jolie and her mother and sister were safe in the United States, he was overwhelmed with emotion. Although *he* was thrilled, the news did cause a major tidal wave within his own home for a while. He had been married for fifteen years, and it was understandable that this news made his wife feel quite threatened, scared, and angry.

"Does he want to see Jolie?" Larry asked me.

"Of course, but his wife's having a hard time with it."

"Did she know he had a daughter in Vietnam?"

"Yes, right from the beginning," I told him, "but you can see her concern. She's naturally wondering what new demands this turn of events will make on their lives."

"Do they have children?"

"A son, I understand," I told Larry.

"Well, think about it. She has no idea what to expect from Diep, for one thing. How will it affect their financial situation, for example? Will he feel obliged to support Jolie? Her mother? Take care of Jolie's education?

"Is she upset with you for starting the whole thing?" he added.

"Yes, she is, and I can't blame her. Apparently Jolie's father is feeling lots of guilt. At this point, the sky's the limit as far as what he wants to do for Jolie and Diep."

"So his wife just doesn't know what to expect?"

"True, although I don't think she begrudges him helping Jolie. Not at all. She sounds like a nice woman. I had a long talk with her when he put her on the phone this evening, and I suspect she's just afraid of having her marriage disrupted."

"You're sort of caught in the middle, aren't you?" Larry put his arm around me.

"Sure am. I feel so sorry for all of them. It's sticky."

"All of these unforeseen dramatic developments," Larry said.

"Can you imagine how *Diep* feels about all of this right about now? If she sees him again, it's bound to shake her up," I told him.

"Well, having a father was apparently very important to Jolie. I have such a warm, paternal feeling toward the girls myself, I can really identify with Jolie's dad on this."

I understood what he meant; after Larry and I had married, his former wife had requested that Larry give her husband permission to adopt their two daughters. This had been traumatic for Larry, but he went along with it in his children's best interests. As it turned out, he did not see his daughters again until they were adults, so he could well understand what a father might feel under these circumstances.

After my first conversation with Jolie's father, I went to the Nguyen home. I had already told Diep and Jolie about my conversation with the couple and had given Jolie her dad's phone number. He and his wife lived in a small community on the eastern seaboard, were well established and quite comfortable financially. The town in which they had lived for many years was so small that everyone knew how loud his neighbors snored, and neither of the couple's families knew anything about Diep or Jolie.

"This kind of news would simply kill my mother or his," Jolie's stepmother said tearfully. "They are so ultra-conservative that even the *idea* would just devastate them!"

"Did you ever think that Jolie would someday turn up?" I asked her.

"Not after all these years," she said. "Of course I'm relieved that she's all right and safe, but it came as such an unexpected shock!"

"Does your son know?" I asked.

"Yes, and he's taken it rather casually, under the circumstances. I think he's a bit curious, in fact. As for me, I feel protective that my child not be cut out of anything that is due him. You can't blame me for that. I want my husband to help with Jolie's education, naturally, but . . ."

"This is going to be hard on Jeanie, too, who hasn't any idea of where her father is right now. I think that Diep was truly abandoned by that man," I said.

"Well, of course we'll do whatever we can for *both* girls," she assured me. "He and I have already talked about this, and there's no way that Jeanie will be left out."

It was that information that I was anxious to impart to the Nguyens. Jeanie's large dark eyes conveyed very little as the four of us talked around their kitchen table. It seemed that Diep did, indeed, know where Jeanie's father was living, but for reasons of her own she chose not to attempt any contact.

"Have you ever tried to reach him?" I asked her.

"Yes. He has daughters. He hurt badly and so crippled," she said. "I no want to write him or contact him." It was said with that emphasis I often heard in her voice, a this-is-the-way-it-is *period* tone.

"Where's Jolie?" I asked when I suddenly realized that she had disappeared as we talked.

"Probably in her room," Jeanie said softly. "This confuse my sister. She don't know how to feel."

"I don't know how to feel either," Diep said. She held her hands clasped in front of her on the table and stared at them. "I never stopped caring for him," she said. "I dreamed that one day he see his daughter, and that I have a picture of them together, and that maybe he do good for his daughter and give her education. I dream of that. . . ."

"There are thousands of Vietnamese women with the same dream, aren't there?" I said. Diep nodded slowly. "I don't want to make trouble for his wife. I think he always still cared for us, though. He was good to me. He loved Jolie and Jeanie when they were babies. I know this."

We went into the living room, and Jolie soon joined us. Her eyes were red from crying. She experienced wide swings of feeling, from joy at discovering her father at last to anger over his abandoning her. She was quiet, and Diep kept looking nervously at her as we sat in their living room together.

"I will call him and say, 'Hello. I'm the daughter you

forget seventeen years ago,' " Jolie said at last, in a choked voice.

"No, no!" Diep shook her head. "Not to make him feel any more guilt," she said. I sensed her maternal protectiveness for Jolie, her concern and sadness for this child who had always felt rejection so acutely.

"I believe he's a good man," I said at last. "He's sincere, and he truly wants to do whatever he can for all of you—even Jeanie, who isn't his own child."

"He *is* a good man," agreed Diep. "I always knew . . ."

"Then I will go to him and he will tell everyone that he is my father," Jolie said. *"Everyone* will know at last."

For a moment I didn't comprehend her meaning. Then I realized that her dream of being acknowledged, of having her own father claim her and love her and want her, was at the core of her being.

"We have to move on this slowly, patiently," I cautioned. "Many other lives are involved now. People could be hurt."

"I've been hurt," Jolie said softly. "I've been hurt all my lifetime."

"Be patient and wait and see," her mother said comfortingly.

When Diep later phoned and said that Jolie's dad and his wife were coming out in April, I determined to make this go as smoothly for everyone as I could. (I had not overlooked the anxiety in Diep's voice.)

I made a couple of trips to the Nguyens just before the visit of Jolie's father. Each time I found Diep anxious, worried about Jolie, and concerned that she and the man's wife might not get along (Diep wanted very much to be friends with the woman). I found Jolie nervous one moment and overjoyed the next.

Diep admitted to "feeling very emotional" about seeing the man whom she had loved for over three years in Vietnam. "But no matter what I feel," she said philosophically, "I will not cry. You must understand the Vietnamese way: You do not show your true feelings, but smile no matter what you feel inside. What is that American song? 'Laughing on the outside . . .'? That's it."

Jolie's father was a gentle man who sincerely wanted to keep things in balance and make everyone at ease. His wife was extremely attractive, vivacious, and equally anxious that things go well. With an admitted temper and excitable nature, she had a rough assignment here. She pulled it off admirably, as did Diep. Perhaps only Larry and I and Diep's children had any idea of what this meant for Diep. She had carried far more than the man's photo with her all those years when her life was so miserable and seemed so hopeless. Meeting him again was to end that dream as the others had been fulfilled.

Jolie's father had an opportunity most returning American servicemen would never have: He could try to make amends and compensate in some measure for his child's suffering, and he was enthusiastic and eager to do so.

The afternoon came when Larry and I met the couple at the hotel near the airport and had them follow us in their rented car to Diep's home. No sooner had we parked the cars in front than Diep came out of the house, grinning and laughing and greeting all of us. I knew what she was feeling, I believe, and I certainly knew what the man and his wife might be experiencing as well. When Jolie came into the living room to meet her father for the first time, he hugged her warmly, and she began to cry. After what her mother had said about "the Vietnamese way," I knew this was doubly humiliating for Jolie.

But they laughed, too, and took many pictures. Then came two days of touring together through San Francisco, with luncheons and dinners out, and a nice visit at our home one evening. It went well, and when we said our good-byes to the couple that last evening, Jolie clung to her father with the desperation of a child who has been lost. I recall standing by our cars in the darkened lot next to a restaurant, Jolie and her father in a silent embrace. I wondered then about the hundreds of Amerasian children still in Vietnam who would have given anything for this experience.

I also realized that fresh in Jolie's memory were the numerous Amerasians who—like herself not so long ago— would *always* be mocked and ridiculed, who would never have the opportunities or protection of their countrymen. That's war, they say; it has always been that way, and when there is war, there will always be children unclaimed by either country. But now at least Jolie is "claimed."

As for her father's wife, today she laughs at past anxieties and has accepted both girls.

"Diep and her daughters are the survivors," a director with Church World Services told me recently. "The refugees who make it over here, who manage to become employed and hold down jobs and go to school, they are the exceptional ones who have learned survival skills and will succeed."

I had read the statistics about the vast numbers of refugees from Southeast Asia who stay on the welfare rolls, who become reclusive and give up, who even commit suicide.

"Your lady had something special," the director told me. "First, she had the courage to withstand anything that life dealt her, determined to see it through, to hang on to her dream. Then"—she smiled at me and winked—"she was, by an odd coincidence of fate, put in contact with someone else who did not understand what giving up meant, either. You're both survivors."

"The three of them marvel at our freedom," I told her. "Not long after their arrival, the girls were with me when a neighbor called over and said that he had an injured squirrel in his backyard. Knowing of my love for animals, he wondered if I wanted to catch the squirrel and see if I could administer to it.

"The girls were fascinated. They might have believed that my intention was to catch the creature and eat it, but they watched curiously as I donned heavy gloves—the squirrel had already attempted to bite my neighbor—and carefully caught the animal and placed him in a cage.

"It was immediately obvious that he had a spinal injury, and I held little hope for the poor thing. With the girls as interested company, I drove the wounded creature to a nearby wildlife emergency hospital. At the time, I didn't think about the effect this might have on my two girls from Vietnam. They seemed transfixed as a white-garbed attendant came to gently carry the animal into an examination room.

"When we left, the girls said nothing as we drove toward home. 'He was shot by someone,' I told them. 'We have an appreciation for wild animals around here. At least, most of us do. Killing an animal for the pleasure of it is frowned on; it's against the law.'

"The girls were still quiet, perhaps thinking about this. Then Jeanie said solemnly in clear and perfect English: 'In Vietnam, you can kill *anything,* but you can't leave the country!' "

Jeanie is self-driven, ambitious, analytical, musical, and determined to succeed and be wealthy and independent. Deeply sensitive, with great familial loyalty, she takes life

seriously and probably had more frequent bouts of homesickness for the land she left behind than her sister. Jolie,
on the other hand, immediately accepted pizza and hot
dogs, is very close to her mother, and has dreams of one
day being a mother herself.

They are so different. Sibling bickering still goes on,
but underlying it there is a deep and unquestionable devotion.

One afternoon recently, I was locking up my office at
the college when I heard laughter coming from a corridor
somewhere nearby.

I did not pay much attention at first. Few students were
on campus, as it was late in the day, and when the laughter
continued—high, delighted, and so joyous—I walked
around the corridor to see who it was. A group of girls
were in the courtyard directly below.

At first I did not recognize them, but soon I saw it was
Jeanie, Jolie, and two of their new Vietnamese friends
having a happy, animated discussion punctuated by laughter.

They did not see me as I stood there in the upper bal-
cony near the corridor, watching the girls in the courtyard
below me enjoying the warm fall afternoon and each other.
I won't try to describe my feeling of gratitude that day and
how I kept seeing them in my mind as I drove home. They
were so happy and free.

Once, before they had purchased their used car, Diep
phoned to say that her bicycle had a flat tire. Larry and I
made the trip to her home, and after Larry had repaired
the tire, Diep had to leave for work. We wanted to drive
her, but she pointed out that she would need the bicycle
to return home.

A few minutes after she had gone, we happened to take
the freeway, which runs parallel to the road Diep was trav-

eling. There she was, bent forward with purpose as she rode along to MacDonald's, and once again I felt a surge of happiness and pride for her. I can only guess what she might be thinking when she rides alone and free, without police checkpoints along the way. That image of her is another of my "mental Polaroids."

The mother who wrote to me so many letters ago, who was tormented that her precious children had no future, now sees her daughters attend college as full-time students, pulling in 4.0 grade-point averages and working at jobs as well. The final part of her dream has come true.

Diep still works at MacDonald's making hamburgers. She smiles a lot these days. For so many months she and her girls rode their bicycles to work in all kinds of weather from their home across from the cemetery, proud to be self-sufficient and independent. Now that they have a car (which runs most of the time), they spend less time on their bikes, but the humility they brought with them to this country is still there, as well as the memories of deprivation and hunger.

With the help once again of the people from St. Andrew's Church, Diep was able to sponsor her sister Minh and nephew Freddy in the fall of 1986. Now the family is all together. It is interesting to note that Freddy enrolled in college within a week of arriving here. He, too, is a gifted student, taking engineering and advanced math classes, and he also works twenty hours a week. He is cheerful and, like Jolie, loves pizza and video games and has all the self-discipline required of "A" students.

Today I believe more fervently than ever in not giving up on a dream. I think that although life may hold few promises and the realist plays it safe in not having great expectations, accomplishment is still much sweeter when one has tenaciously clung to a dream, refusing to let go.

Dreams kept Diep and me alive. We each had trials and ordeals to contend with and conquer, but the dream of survival always sustained us.

Sometimes it still does not seem real that Diep and her children are in this country safe and free, that it has all come to pass. When the girls first found Larry's old guitar the day after they arrived here, they took turns playing it and singing lilting Vietnamese folk songs, accompanied that warm summer evening by the frogs in our pond. I felt awe and disbelief as I listened to their soft young voices sing those beautiful and romantic Vietnamese songs. It struck me then that even after years of hunger, exhaustion, terror, some experiences too horrible to describe, after schooling that condemned Americans and America's values *and* Vietnam's old regime, Jeanie and Jolie could still recall those beautiful songs of the Vietnamese past.

Perhaps there is a lesson to be learned from those people of the earth whose history has been marred by war or persecution. While we may ask ourselves questions about human endurance, about the tests of the human spirit, we see there is something infinitely resilient and life affirming in the soul of the survivor.

Although those three hundred letters that passed between Diep and me for nearly two decades formed a paper bridge, like most bridges ours rested at each end on a solid base. The letters between us have stopped forever, but the friendship and affection they fostered will last us all of our lives.

An Update

On June 15th, 1990, Nguyen thi Mai Cat (Jeanie) received her B.S. degree in engineering, with honors, from the University of California at Davis. Her sister, Nguyen thi Mai Uyen, whom we call Jolie, will earn her degree—also in engineering—from Davis in June of 1991, thus fulfilling Diep's dearest dream as expressed in her earliest letters to me so long ago.

Their family now includes their attractive Aunt Minh, Diep's sister, who arrived in the United States two years after them with her son Freddy, a brilliant student at the University of California in Berkeley.

Diep and I do not see each other very often anymore, although we live within ten miles of each other and are more "sisterly" than most blood sisters when we do visit. We are both so busy with our lives. Diep works at three part-time jobs! She has been chosen "Employee of the Month" many times at the MacDonald's that hired her more than four years ago. Her smile is broader now. All three women have completely lost that frightened, anxious and self-conscious demeanor so evident upon their arrival. They have been self-sufficient and self-supporting ever since they left my home.

Larry and I spent over twenty years together, parting in 1987. His personal vision for himself never quite fit the role that was imposed upon him with our marriage; although he was sincere and gave it his very best, now single he is a happier man.

Despite the great sadness associated with some of my life's transitions, I do believe these have been the periods when I've grown the most. I would avoid their pain, of course, if I could, but I welcome their lessons. And when I look at Diep and her daughters, I think that if we are fortunate enough to help someone else find fulfillment and freedom, we become *both* the benefactor and the beneficiary.

I continue to teach at Diablo Valley College and am working on a new novel and film script. My happy situation today is that I have found someone special, a man with whom I'll soon be crossing the new bridges in my life, and I guess that *is* a public announcement.

Jann Jansen